# Anointed But Broken

**What the Enemy Meant for Evil**
**God Meant for Good**

# NIKKI ST.CLAIR

## TRILOGY
### A WHOLLY OWNED SUBSIDIARY OF TBN
PROFESSIONAL PUBLISHING MEETS POWERFUL PROMOTION

*Anointed But Broken*
Trilogy Christian Publishers A Wholly Owned Subsidiary of Trinity Broadcasting Network
2442 Michelle Drive Tustin, CA 92780
Copyright © 2024 by Nikki St.Clair

Rights Department, 2442 Michelle Drive, Tustin, CA 92780.
Trilogy Christian Publishing/TBN and colophon are trademarks of Trinity Broadcasting Network.
Cover design by: Gary Smith
For information about special discounts for bulk purchases, please contact Trilogy Christian Publishing.
Trilogy Disclaimer: The views and content expressed in this book are those of the author and may not necessarily reflect the views and doctrine of Trilogy Christian Publishing or the Trinity Broadcasting Network.
10 9 8 7 6 5 4 3 2 1
Library of Congress Cataloging-in-Publication Data is available.
ISBN: 979-8-88738-539-6
E-ISBN: 979-8-88738-540-2

This book is dedicated to all who have been in a broken place in their life, a place of great despair and agony, for anyone who has been in a state of inner turmoil and confusion about their future. This book is dedicated to all who have struggled with fear and anxiety and worry and doubt. This book is dedicated to all who wanted to give up and quit but, by the grace of God, continued on in the good fight of faith. This book is dedicated to all who have been in a weary place, a desolate place, and a place of despondency that tried to keep them bound and give up on life. This book is dedicated to the strong, courageous souls who, even in the midst of heartache and pain, even in the midst of isolation and utter grief, would not allow their brokenness to hinder them, but instead, the brokenness encouraged them to press on, because you have faith that your purpose is greater than your pain.

The Lord is near to the brokenhearted, and He saves those who are crushed in spirit (Psalm 34:18). Cast all your cares upon Jesus, for He cares for you (1 Peter 5:7). Jesus can heal every broken place in your life if you'll allow Him to do so.

# Table of Contents

# CHAPTER ONE

# Trials and Tribulations

In life, there will be times of testing, difficult times, times when you feel like your life is falling apart, times that are so hard to bear that you feel like giving up. No one is exempt from going through trials. It is in the hard times of life that bring about change in a person's life, whether for good or for bad. Going through hardships can sometimes make you feel stuck. But being stuck in your circumstances is a choice.

Have you ever felt so stuck in a situation that you could not see a way out? Have you ever been so down that you told God, "Lord, I can't take much more of this." Everyone has had moments in their life when it seemed hopeless, but as a believer in Christ, hopelessness is not your destination; victory is. We have the victory through Christ. And keep in mind we are fighting from the place of victory, not trying to obtain victory. "But thanks be to God, who gives us the victory through our Lord Jesus Christ" (1 Corinthians 15:57). The battle that you are in right now has already been won when Jesus died on the cross for you. The Scripture tells us in James 1:2 to count it all joy when you fall into divers temptations, knowing that the trying of your faith works patience.

Trials build character. No matter what your situation looks like, no matter how long you have been in an uncomfortable season in your life, no matter how many times you may have fallen, get back up again and continue on. Do not give up because it is hard. Do not give up because you cannot see a way out with your natural mind. Rely on the Lord to see you through. Lean on Him for strength. Lean on Him for guidance. Let Jesus lead you out of that valley place in your life. Remain joyful in God, even when going through trials. Rest in God. Trust Him that troublesome situations are not permanent but temporary. Do what King David did: he encouraged himself in the Lord (see 1 Samuel 30:6).

Your situation may not have changed yet in the natural, but declare that all is well. Speak things that be not as though they were (Romans 5:17). You will have what you say. Your words have power and can affect your life greatly by what you say (Proverbs 18:21). Words have life. You can bless your life, or you can curse your life by the words you speak. Do not call it the way it is; call it the way you desire it to be.

*"Lord, I don't understand how this situation is going to change, but I trust in You with all my heart. I will not lean on my own*

*understanding. I acknowledge You in all my*
*ways, and I trust in You to direct my path."*

## The Lord Does Not Expect Us to Have It All Figured Out

It is okay to not know. The Lord does not expect us to have it all figured out. If that were the case, we would not need a Savior. But God!

Speak God's Word back to Him. When you declare the Word of God over your situation, that is appropriating (to make use of, to apply) the Word in your life. Be a doer of the Word, and not a hearer only (James 1:22–25). The Word of God is alive and active (Hebrews 4:12). The Word of God gives instruction. God's Word is the answer to every issue we face in life; that is what the Bible is: an instruction manual with the Holy Spirit as our Guide, leading us to Jesus.

In Matthew 24:35, when Jesus spoke the Parable of the Fig Tree, He tells us that heaven and earth will pass away, but His Words will never pass away. How awesome is that?! The Word of God will never go out of existence! The Word will never die; it will live forever! I don't know about you, but that makes my heart glad! What a blessed assurance that God's Word is never changing, never ceasing, and always at work, but you have to work it. If you want God's Word to be effective in your life, you have to apply it to your life. You have to be obedient to the Word, just as Jesus Christ was when He was in the earth—God is the Word. "In the beginning was the Word, and the Word was with God, and the Word was God" (John 1:1). Christ was obedient to the Word even unto His death on the cross (Philippians 2:8).

That is why it is so imperative to sow to the Spirit and not to the flesh. Overthinking is sowing to the flesh. Worry is sowing to the flesh. Anxiety is sowing to the flesh. Anything that you put your energy into, you are sowing into. When you sow to your flesh, will of the flesh reap corruption, but when you sow to the Spirit will of the Spirit reap life everlasting life (see Galatians 6:8).

I am blessed.
(Ephesians 1:3–4; Matthew 5:1–12; Ps. 32:1)

I am chosen by God.
(Ephesians 1:3–6; 1 Peter 2:9; John 15:16)

I am the healed of the Lord.
(Isaiah 53:5; Jeremiah 1:5; 2 Thessalonians 2:14)

I am an overcomer.
(1 John 5:4–5; Philippians 4:13; Revelation 21:7)

I am more than a conqueror.
(Romans 8:37; Revelation 3:21; Revelation 12:11)

I am the head, and not the tail.
(Deuteronomy 28:13; Deuteronomy 15:6; Genesis 22:18)

I am above only, and not beneath.
(Deuteronomy 28:13; Genesis 1:26–28; Luke 10:19)

The Lord always causes me to triumph.
(2 Corinthians 2:14; Psalm 25:2; Proverbs 28:12)

Jesus loves me.
(John 3:16; Ephesians 2:4–7; Romans 5:8)

I am the redeemed of the Lord.
(Psalm 107:2; Isaiah 43:1; Ephesians 1:7–10)

I am delivered.
(Psalm 34:17; Psalm 50:15; 2 Samuel 22)

I am the righteousness of God in Christ Jesus.
(2 Corinthians 5:21; 1 John 3:7; Philippians 3:9)

God is for me.
(Romans 8:31; Matthew 28:30; Psalm 56:9)

*Speak life! (Proverbs 18:21)*

Speaking words of faith activates the power of God in your life. God is faithful to His Word. "...without faith it is impossible to please Him..." (Hebrews 11:6). When you speak the Word of God back to God, you say what the Lord says about you in His Word. All of the promises in the Bible belong to you as a child of the Most High. "For all the promises of God in Him are Yes, and in Him Amen, to the glory of God through us" (2 Corinthians 1:20).

The more you speak faith-filled words, the more your inner man will grow and prosper in God. The Bible is filled with promises from the Father, filled with words of faith, filled with life-giving principles to give you direction and guidance. "Faith comes by hearing..." (Romans 5:17).

That is why it is so important to read God's Word out loud. Speaking God's Word out loud allows it to take root in your spirit, and eventually, those roots will begin to grow. Hearing yourself declare the Word audibly is vital. When you speak the Word out loud, you are speaking *life*. God is a speaking God. In Genesis 1, when God created the heavens and the earth before He created a "thing," He spoke it first. That is what we ought to do: speak it!

Allow God's Word to be spoken out of your mouth. God's Word is life-giving, not just physical life, but spiritual life as well. We are spiritual beings living a natural experience. It has already happened in heaven, but we must declare the Word of God here in the earth to manifest it. And keep this in mind: the only manifestation that we as believers should be involved in is the manifestation of the promises of the Word of God. Any other type of manifesting is witchcraft; it is idolatry and not of God. The manifestation is an indication of the existence, reality, or presence. God reveals Himself through His Word. And since we know that in the beginning was the Word, and the Word was with God, and the Word was God, we know that the Word has always been.

Allow the Word of God to water those roots, and you will flourish like a tree (see Psalm 92:12–15). Jesus is Living Water (see Isaiah 58:11; John 7:37; Isaiah 12:3; Revelation 7:16–17; Revelation 22:1). When you drink of Him (allowing His Word to saturate your life, communing spirit to Spirit), you will never be thirsty. He will water every dry place in your life. Your spirit will be filled with His Water so that when times of testing come, you will have the strength to endure.

The Lord allows trials and tribulations. The question is how we handle the trials and tribulations when they come. Can Jesus trust you in the good times and the bad? Can He trust you when everything in your life is going well and when nothing seems to be working out in your favor? We can always trust God because He does not change, but we change all the time. We say one thing and do another. We break promises. We forget. And sometimes, we are just downright disobedient.

Everything is not going to go our way all the time. We will have bumps in the road. We will have roadblocks that try to take us off course. We will have times of uncertainty; that is when faith comes in. The next time you go through trials and tribulations (and there will be a next time—that is part of life), instead of being filled with hopelessness and despondency, be filled with God's Word. His Word will strengthen you and give you hope. His Word will assure you that Jesus is there right in the midst of your trial, right in the midst of your tribulation, and that He is helping you along the way. You can walk by faith, knowing that the Holy Spirit is guiding you even in times of uncertainty. When you do that, the hard times of life will not overwhelm you because you know you have an Advocate (the Holy Spirit), Who is at work in your situation.

# CHAPTER TWO

# Heeding the Voice of the Holy Spirit

Oftentimes, the situations that we are faced with are because of our own choices. God enables us to have self-control. Lack of self-control gets us out of alignment with the will of God. Every choice we make can affect our circumstances. Making wrong choices will cause God's plan for our life to be held up. Doing things our way instead of heeding the voice of the Holy Spirit will cause us to be delayed. The main reason we try and do things "our way" and not wait on God is out of fear. Being fearful that God will not do what He promised to do or fearful that things will not work out the way you want them to, so you put your hand in it instead of allowing the hand of God to lead you and do things His way. "…not My will, but Yours, be done" (Luke 22:42).

Any time you notice yourself getting ahead of God and wanting to do "things" your way instead of waiting on God, remember—disobedience blocks blessings. The

Lord does not reward disobedience. If you have been living in disobedience to God, choose not to any longer. There is a better way, and it starts with repentance. When you repent, that means that you turn from what you have been doing; you turn away from sin and turn towards the Father. Surrender to God's will and God's way. Let go of everything and everyone that the Lord has told you to let go of. It is time to cut away what is dead in your life: dead attitudes, dead mindsets, dead religion; cut it away. Die to self, what self wants, how self feels. It is time to live in the newness of life. Once you accepted Jesus Christ as your personal Savior, your life changed instantly. Your circumstances may not have changed right away, but the life you knew before you turned to God changed. Your name was written in the *Lamb's Book of Life*, you became a child of the Most High God, and you were sealed (to cover, secure, eternally binding) with the Blood of Jesus. We have a covenant with the Father, through His Son, Jesus Christ, by acknowledging His death on the cross and our acceptance of Him as our Lord and Savior.

Now, it is up to you to walk out your salvation. Jesus Christ did everything for us when He went to the cross for us. He has already overcome everything that you will go through in your life. Refuse to allow any trial, any setback, any hurt, or any tribulation to keep you down. When the testing of your faith comes, go through it with God. Keep Christ at the center of your life. Be obedient to God. Spend time with Him in His Word. Have faith in Him. Trust Him.

Lean on Him. Worship Him in spirit and in truth (see John 4:24). We serve the One True Living God. As His child, we can move forward in life, no matter what comes against us. Tribulation is not meant to break you; it is meant to build you up in the Lord, to build up your hope in God. "...tribulation produces perseverance; and perseverance, character; and character, hope" (Romans 5:3–4).

The Lord never said that we would not have tribulation in this world. Jesus tells us in John 16:33 that we will have tribulation, but to be of good cheer, for He has overcome the world. You can be encouraged and comforted by the Holy Spirit because Christ has already overcome the world. He conquered it all! The enemy has been defeated, and the Lord Jesus Christ prevails! Forever!

God does not expect us to do everything right or to never make mistakes. As long as we are in our earthly body, we will make mistakes and continually need to repent. We must live a life of repentance. God already knows that we will miss the mark. So, do not ever think that you have to be perfect for God to love you because only Christ is perfect. God loves you because of Who He is, not because of how good you are.

The Lord desires for us to be obedient to Him, to stay close to Him (remain in fellowship with) and trust Him. When you seek first the kingdom of God and His righteousness, you will never lose. A relationship with the Lord Jesus Christ brings joy, peace, comfort, protection, and so many other wonderful blessings. In Him, you will be brought into the fullness of life (see Colossians 2:9–10).

> *"But seek first the kingdom of God, and His righteousness, and all these things shall be added to you."*
>
> **Matthew 6:33**

Seeking the Lord has to be a habit in the life of the believer. Every day we should be seeking the Lord, seeking the Holy Spirit. When we seek the Holy Spirit, we are seeking God's perfect will. But it requires listening to that still, small voice. It requires opening our minds and our hearts to Him. Heeding the voice of the Holy Spirit is essential in our Christian walk (to heed is to pay close attention to; to listen to and consider). By seeking the Holy Spirit, we gain truth into all things. The Holy Spirit is our Teacher. He brings all things to our remembrance (John 14:26).

For instance, have you ever been praying for someone and stumbled over a Scripture that the Lord put in your mouth? When you stumbled, it was because you were thinking with your natural mind, but when you yield yourself to the Holy Spirit, He reminds you of what His Word says. It is not of our own doing but the unction of the Holy Spirit. First John 2:20 (KJV) says, "But ye have an unction from the Holy One, and ye know all things."

The New King James Version refers to unction as an anointing. Every born-again believer is anointed by God.

20

But not every believer opens themselves up to the Holy Spirit to use the anointing God has placed on their life. Each of us has a gift(s) [talents] from the Father. Some have five talents. Some have two talents. Some may have only one talent (see Matthew 25:14–30). We all have purpose in God. We all have something special and significant that we are to accomplish in the earth for the glory of the Father, to bring lost souls to Christ, and to grow God's kingdom. We are all here in this world to do the work of the Lord in some way or another. Jesus Christ desires to live His life through us so that the Father may be glorified in the Son.

Are there dreams that God has spoken to your heart? Are there visions that you have allowed to die because it did not work out the first time? Is there something that you know that the Lord has called you to do for His glory that you have been sitting on? If God gave you the vision, do not waste it, do not doubt the purpose God has placed in your heart—go after it! Go after your dreams, go after your desires, and do it all for the glory of God. It may take a while to accomplish, it may be hard, and there will be times when you want to quit, but press on! It is in the pressing times of life that the Lord is doing a great work in you. Growth hurts. But what hurts even more is not living out the purpose and plan of God for your life. Refuse to spend your life in regret of who you could have been and what you could have done, all because you gave up. Keep working towards what the Lord has called you to do. Keep being your best and doing your best. Be not weary in well doing (Galatians 6:9). Thank God for His grace (divine assistance) to accomplish every task you set out to do. His grace is sufficient (2 Corinthians 12:9).

Be encouraged that God is with you in your struggles. He is fighting your battles (Deuteronomy 3:21). He goes before you, making your crooked places straight (Isaiah 45:2). He prepares the way for you, making your way prosperous. You have an Advocate, a Comforter, and a Helper. The Holy Spirit is your help. Through Christ, you can do all things because He strengthens you (Philippians 4:13). We are more than conquerors through Him who loved us (Romans 8:37). Allow the Spirit of the Lord to help you to conquer your fears, conquer your doubts, and conquer those nagging thoughts that you do not have what it takes to succeed.

The Father created you for His good pleasure. Start seeing yourself the way God sees you. He calls you an overcomer, blessed, prosperous, equipped, strong, and courageous. You've got what it takes to accomplish every dream the Lord has set before you because you have the great I Am living on the inside of you. The Lord can do anything, but He cannot fail. The Word He spoke to your heart will not fail; His Word never fails (Joshua 21:45).

Isaiah 55:11 encourages us that God's Word will not return to Him void. But it will accomplish what He pleases... God's Word does not change. God's Word is constant. His Word is sustaining. His Word is effective.

God's Word is always active! Take God at His Word— He watches over His Word to fulfill it (Jeremiah 1:12, AMP).

Either you believe God, or you don't. There are no two ways about it. Look at the story of the Virgin Mary, how the angel of the Lord told her that she would conceive and give birth to a child Who would be called the Son of the Most High God, Who would reign forever, and Whose kingdom will never end. That seemed impossible in the natural. Mary was even perplexed at what the angel had spoken to her because she was a virgin. But nevertheless, Mary believed God, and she believed His Word to be fulfilled. That is the same kind of faith that we must have about the promises that God has spoken over our lives. It may seem farfetched, it may seem impossible, it may seem out there, but faith is not what you see—it is what you do not see.

Faith in God can move mountains in your life. You can sail to great heights when you trust in God and believe on Him—let go of your doubts. Trust God with your whole heart. Do what is necessary to accomplish your dreams. He will be with you every step of the way; leading you; guiding you, and directing your steps. As you move, He will move. As you work, He will work. You can have great faith, but without works, your faith is dead (James 2:26).

Work towards your God-given destiny. Let go of the fear of failure. Fear is a lie! But faith is the *Truth*. Without Faith in God, it is impossible to please Him. Let's please the Lord in all we do, and most importantly, let's please

Him by having unwavering faith in Him. Believe the Word. Trust the Word. Have faith in the Word. God's Word is His bond (binding agreement, a covenant, a promise), and it cannot be broken. God is faithful. "God is not a man, that He should lie, Nor a son of man, that He should repent. Has He said, and will He not do? Or has He spoken, and will He not make it good?" (Numbers 23:19). Heeding the voice of the Holy Spirit will keep your foot from stumbling. Heeding the voice of the Holy Spirit will keep sin from you. Heeding the voice of the Holy Spirit gives you the ability to know things you would not otherwise know. Every day when you wake up and pray before God, thank the Lord for the Holy Spirit. Thank Him for His presence (see Romans 12:1). Invite the Holy Spirit into your home, invite Him into your day-to-day life, and invite Him into your heart. Allow the Holy Spirit to make His home in you. Present your body to Him as a living sacrifice. Allow the Holy Spirit to speak to your heart.

First Kings 19:12 says that the voice of the Lord is a still, small voice. The Lord speaks with clarity. When the Holy Spirit speaks, He is not loud, but He speaks in such a way to get your attention, where you know it is His voice speaking to you at that moment. He speaks directly to your heart. He will speak to your situation in such a profound way that there is no denying that He is Who He says He is.

The Holy Spirit is a great gift in the life of the believer. He can be in all places at the same time. He can speak to you and the person next to you and the person next to them all at the same time in a very unique way. He knows us so well. He knows our struggles. He knows our hurt and our pain. He knows us intimately.

I can recall a time when I was feeling extremely restless. I was not sleepy or tired, but my spirit was restless. I had an unfulfilled longing that frustrated me greatly. Then, the Holy Spirit brought to my remembrance a word of encouragement that I had recently heard on a ministry program. And I remember hearing the Holy Spirit say, "Jesus can heal you every place you hurt." When I heard that in my spirit, I collapsed to the floor and cried like a baby. I was incredibly depressed because I was not living up to my full potential in God. I allowed the cares of the world to get me down. Instead of focusing on Jesus and His finished works on the cross, I focused on myself. I focused on how stuck I felt. I focused on how hopeless I felt. I focused on my situation and not on the Lord. I allowed myself to be led by my emotions, which always leads to distress. But when I heard the Lord's voice, I knew there was still hope for me. I knew that God had not forgotten about me, even though I had put Him to the wayside. Oftentimes, when I struggled with depression, I did not pray or seek God. I allowed my despondency to have its way in my life instead of allowing the Lord to have His way. I was weighed down by the spirit of heaviness, but God!

We must cast down imaginations (see 2 Corinthians 10:4–6, KJV). The Amplified Version says, "We are destroying sophisticated arguments and every exalted *and* proud thing that sets itself up against the [true] knowledge of God…" We must bring every thought into captivity to the obedience of Christ. In other words, make your thoughts obey the Word. Make your thoughts obey the Truth of Who God is and what His Word promises. As I mentioned earlier, confess God's Word out loud. Hear yourself speak the Word so that it becomes so embedded in your spirit that when the evil one attacks your mind, you have God's Word in your heart and on your lips, ready to quench (to put out, to extinguish, to put down) every fiery dart he throws at you (Ephesians 6:16). "…For out of the abundance of the heart his mouth speaks" (Luke 6:45). "For as he thinks in his heart, so is he" (Proverbs 23:70).

You do not have to allow every little thought to settle in your mind—Jesus Christ settled it all on the cross with finality. *"It is finished!"* You do not have to allow every wrong thought to get down in your spirit. You do not have to allow wrong thoughts to take root. Wrong thoughts are not planted by God. Refuse to allow wrong thinking to grow in your life, cut it off at the root! Just because you think it, it does not mean you have to say it. Ask the Lord to set a guard over your mouth and keep watch over your lips (see Psalm 141:3–4).

Abide in God. Be pruned by the Spirit of the Lord. He is our constant Gardener. Love the Lord with all your mind (Matthew 22:37). Trust in Him to align your thoughts with His thoughts. First Corinthians 2:16 encourages us that we have the mind of Christ. Any thought that comes against the truth of God's Word, renounce it in the Name of Jesus. Allow the Holy Spirit to cut away every thought that is in opposition to what His Word promises. When wrong thoughts come, there will be times to just ignore them, and then there will be times to speak against them, especially when the thoughts are rampant. Know that it is the enemy who is afflicting your mind; that is his place of attack, the mind. Any time the enemy attacks your mind with wrong thoughts, with wrong imaginations, say the opposite of his lies.

## Try this:

*The devil says you're sick, say, "By the stripes that fell on Jesus' back, I am healed."*

*The devil says you're broke, say, "The Lord is my Provider. He is Jehovah-Jireh. My God provides all my needs according to His riches in glory in Christ Jesus. I'm rich."*

*The devil says you're going to die, say, "My life and the length of my days are in the Lord's hands. The number of my days He will fulfill."*

*The devil says you're not loved, say, "Jesus loves me, for the Bible tells me so."*

*The devil says you're weak, say, "I am strong in the Lord and in the power of His might."*

*The devil says your best days are over, say, "My latter day shall be greater than my former day."*

*The devil says you're not equipped, say, "I can do all things through Christ Who strengthens me."*

This is a war that we are in. We are not fighting against flesh and blood, so we cannot use natural weapons to combat the enemy. This is a spiritual fight that we are in. Therefore, our weapons must be spiritual. The Word of God is our weapon. The Word of God is our sword against every attack of the enemy. Put your armor on! Gear up! You've got a devil to fight, and how you defeat him in your life is by declaring, decreeing, and confessing the Word of God out loud with confidence and boldness.

Cast down wrong imaginations. Make your thoughts obey the Word. "How?" you ask. By declaring the Word. By confessing the Word of God. By meditating on His Word day and night. A wrong mindset is fruitlessness. But if you abide in Christ, you will bear much fruit (ripe fruit, good for the picking). Abiding in Christ allows the same mind that is in Christ to be in you (Philippians 2:5–11).

The voice of the Holy Spirit gives hope in a hopeless situation. The voice of the Holy Spirit gives life to a dead thing. The voice of the Holy Spirit convicts and corrects. The voice of the Holy Spirit renews faith in God that was temporarily lost. The voice of the Holy Spirit gives assurance that the Lord sees you right where you are. He is El-Roi (The God Who sees me). God sees you, even in your wilderness, He sees you (Genesis 16:13–14).

# CHAPTER THREE

## Wilderness

The wilderness is a place of desolation, an unsettling place, a place of hardship, a place of opposition. Many times, when going through a "wilderness experience," you will be faced with spiritual warfare. Spiritual warfare is a fight for your soul. A fight of good versus evil. There are evil (demonic) forces (evil spirits) sent from the pit of hell to stop the purpose and plan of God in the life of the believer. "…from the days of John the Baptist until now the kingdom of heaven suffers violence, and the violent take it by force" (Matthew 11:12).

The wilderness is no place anyone desires to be. When in the wilderness, you may have times of uncertainty and apprehension. There may be uneasiness, a fearful expectation, a feeling of dread or alarm. It is often a place of great inner turmoil. Uncertainty is a constant fear of "what if." Uncertainty brings about reasoning. Reasoning is of the devil. The devil always attacks with what he might do. But he has no power to do anything unless God first gives him permission. (*Remember the story of Job?*)

When Moses led the Israelites out of slavery in Egypt and across the Red Sea, they did not immediately go into the land that God promised them—Canaan. They spent forty years living in the wilderness. A journey that should have taken eleven days took them forty years. The reason they were in the wilderness for so long was due to their attitude and their disobedience to God. Sometimes, we are the reason for being in a wilderness experience for a long period of time. The children of Israel murmured and complained. They rebelled against God. They were disobedient. They feared man when they should have feared (have awe-filled reverence) for the Lord. Fear of man is a trap of the enemy (Proverbs 29:25), but trusting in the Lord is the ultimate safety. God is our Defender. He is our Refuge. We can run to Him, and He will hide us under the shadow of the Almighty.

> *"He that dwelleth in the secret place of the most High shall abide under the shadow of the Almighty. I will say of the LORD, He is my refuge and my fortress: my God; in him I will trust. Surely he shall deliver thee from the snare of the fowler, and from the noisome pestilence. He shall cover thee with his feathers, and under his wings shalt thou trust: his truth shall be thy shield and buckler. Thou shall not be afraid for the terror by night; nor for the arrow that flieth by day; Nor for the pestilence that walketh in darkness; nor for the destruction that*

*wasteth at noonday. A thousand shall fall
at thy side, and ten thousand at thy right
hand; but it shall not come nigh thee. Only
with thine eyes shalt thou behold and see
the reward of the wicked. Because thou hast
made the LORD, which is my refuge, even
the most High, thy habitation; There shall
no evil befall thee, neither shall any plague
come nigh thy dwelling. For he shall give
his angels charge over thee, to keep thee in
all thy ways. They shall bear thee up in their
hands, lest thou dash thy foot against a stone.
Thou shalt tread upon the lion and adder: the
young lion and the dragon shalt thou trample
under feet. Because he hath set his love upon
me, therefore will I deliver him: I will set him
on high, because he hath known my name. He
shall call upon me, and I will answer him: I
will be with him in trouble; I will deliver him,
and honour him. With long life will I satisfy
him, and shew him my salvation."*

**Psalm 91 (KJV)**

Fear of man says you doubt Who God is. Where there is doubt, there is unbelief. Fear is the opposite of faith. Fear will keep you stuck. Just like the Israelites were stuck on the mountain in the wilderness for all those years, we, too, can stay stuck in our "wilderness" when we do not trust God. Living in obstinacy to the Lord always leads to a standstill. When we are obstinate to God, we are stubborn; we choose our way instead of allowing God to have His way. God will not force you to do anything. The Holy

Spirit will instruct you. The Holy Spirit will correct you. The Holy Spirit will steer you in the right direction, but when you are not willing to obey, when you are not willing to yield to Him, He will let you have your way. You will go around the same mountain, over and over and over again, until you are willing to yield to the Lord.

Refusing to yield to the Lord is deliberate sin. It is willful disobedience. Romans 6:23 reminds us, "…the wages of sin is death…" Ask yourself, "What am I willing to 'pay' (wages) to continue in sin, to continue in disobedience?" Ask yourself, "Is it worth it to go my own way instead of the way God desires to lead me?" There is nothing better than yielding yourself to the Holy Spirit. There is nothing better than God's purpose, plan, and will for your life. It's God's way, or God's way, period.

God's way is always the best way. His plan is always the best plan. His will for you is always for good. Being in the will of God is where you want to be. Being outside of the will of God is a recipe for disaster; nothing good will come from it. Even when the repercussions are not immediate, they will happen eventually. "Do not be deceived: God is not mocked: for whatever a man sows, that he will also reap" (Galatians 6:7).

Sowing disobedience reaps calamity. But sowing obedience reaps blessings. When you choose to be obedient to the Lord, there is a peace, because you know that God's will is at hand—the Lord gives us free will. He will not force anything on you. The choice of obedience is up to you. When you say to the Lord that you submit to His authority, you also submit to His will.

Submission is an act of love. When you love God, you keep His commandments (John 14:15), you obey. Even when you do not "feel" like it, you do it anyway because God says so. Just like a parent expects their children to obey because the parent knows what is best for the child, that is the same way God is. He expects us to obey Him. It is His desire for us to obey Him as His children because He knows what is best for us, and He desires to keep us from situations that will lead us down the wrong road and could potentially harm us. He will teach us; He will guide us; He will correct us; He will encourage us, and He will enable us by His Spirit to be obedient to Him, but He will not force us. Ultimately, the choice is up to us.

Obedience to God tells Him that you submit to His authority in your life. Obedience tells God that you trust His will and His way and that you will adhere (to stick to, to stay attached, to remain devoted) to Him in and out of season. It's about faith in God. Having faith in God and taking Him at His Word will encourage you to remain obedient to Him.

All throughout Scripture, the Bible talks about faith. We must live by faith. Anything we do in life for the kingdom of God must be done by faith. The Bible says: *it is by faith we understand.*

*"By faith we understand that the worlds were framed by the word of God [...] By faith Abel offered to God a more excellent sacrifice than Cain [...] By faith Enoch was taken away so that he did not see death [...] By faith Noah, being divinely warned of things not yet seen, moved with godly fear [...] By faith Abraham obeyed when he was called..."*

**Hebrews 11:3–5; 7–8**

You cannot please God without faith (Hebrews 11:6). That is what the devil is after—your faith. Stay in faith, no matter what is going on around you, no matter how you feel, no matter what, have faith in the Lord. Your faith is a powerful weapon against the enemy. Get this down in your spirit right now: the devil is a liar! Everything he says is a lie. The enemy's number one goal is to steal the believer's faith. And it is in the wilderness experiences of life when your faith is tested the most. But do not lose heart, the devil is defeated. The more you stay obedient to the Lord, the more you will trust Him, the more you trust Him, the more your faith will grow, and the more evident it will become that the enemy cannot succeed against you because Christ is in you. "But we overcome the enemy by the blood of the Lamb, and by the word of our testimony" (Revelation 12:11).

# CHAPTER FOUR

# Overcoming Fear and Anxiety

The spirit of fear is one of torment. When you are tormented, you are in anguish, worried, and afflicted in your mind. To be tormented is to worry excessively, to be incessantly annoyed mentally. The purpose of torment is to disturb your peace. Worry is not of God. It is not God's will for you to live in torment of any kind.

Second Timothy 1:7 says, "For God has not given us a spirit of fear; but of power and of love and of a sound mind." When fear comes, it comes to cause a disturbance (mental or emotional imbalance or disorder) in your thinking, so you cannot think clearly. Consider the mental illnesses that affect millions of Americans; it is caused by a spirit of fear. Some of the mental health issues connected to fear are anxiety, excessive worry, obsessive compulsion, hallucinations, and so on.

Fear is a disease. What I mean by that is a DIS-EASE

is an abnormal condition; to live in a perpetual state of fear is not normal. To be diseased is to carry a condition or tendency regarded as harmful. Disease is impairment. To be impaired in the mind is to lack function. All of the connections to fear cause dysfunction. Dysfunction is the failure to display the characteristics or fulfill beneficial purposes. Think about that, the failure to fulfill beneficial purposes.

We all have a God-given purpose, but if there is a dysfunction in our minds, if there is an illness that comes against our minds, the purposes of God are delayed or held up. Being able to think clearly is essential, but fear causes confusion, and confusion causes distress. Where there is constant distress, the mind is divided; and there is confusion in the mind. God is not the author of confusion but of peace (1 Corinthians 14:33). The Lord desires for His children to be at peace. It is difficult to be at peace when the mind is divided and distressed. Any time that you begin to be tormented by the spirit of fear, remind yourself that God is not the author of confusion but of peace. Remind yourself that the spirit of fear does not come from God.

It is not the Lord's will for you to live in fear. Fear is a spirit of evil, a spirit of wickedness, a spirit of affliction. Fear is a tactic of the enemy used to paralyze you so that you will not achieve God's purpose for your life. Fear robs you of joy. Fear attempts to destroy your faith in God. Fear is a devourer.

As mentioned earlier, "…faith comes by hearing, and hearing by the word of God" (Romans 10:17). The Word of God is nourishment. His Word feeds us. God's Word feeds your faith. His Word causes you to grow (spiritually). "…Man shall not live by bread alone, but by every word that proceeds from the mouth of God" (Matthew 4:4). Just like it is essential to partake of natural food on a daily basis to continue on living, it is essential to partake of the Word of God on a daily basis. God's Word is the True Bread. Jesus Christ is Living Bread. His Word feeds. His Word grows us spiritually. His Word cultivates. His Word sustains. God's Word is life-changing, life-giving, and life-sustaining (see Psalm 119). Jesus Christ is the Bread of Life (John 6:22–58).

Without daily feeding on the Word of God, we cannot grow in God. Without daily feeding on the Word of God, we have no life, no true life that is. To merely exist and not really live is no life at all. But Jesus came that we may have life and life abundantly (John 10:10). Feeding on the Word of God (feeding on the knowledge of Who God is) must be a priority in the life of the believer. Without it, we will perish; without it, we are insufficient. But when we have confidence through Christ toward God, our sufficiency comes from Him. Apart from Christ, we are insufficient, but in Him, we have been made sufficient (see 2 Corinthians 3:4–6).

The spirit of fear causes malnutrition. It starves your faith. As soon as you begin to feed your faith through God's

Word, which are His promises, fear sets out to devour (to eat up greedily, to consume, to destroy, and to waste) God's Truth that you have heard and fill your heart and your mind with lies. To be malnourished is to starve for lack of food. God's Word is food. When you partake of the Word on a daily basis, you are feeding your mind, your body, and your spirit. Your mind is being renewed by the Word. Your body is a temple for the Holy Spirit to dwell. Your spirit is at one with God's Spirit. Your being (your existence) wants to be one with God, but if it is being malnourished continuously with untruths, eventually it will separate itself from God and starve to death. "...in Him we live and move and have our being..." (Acts 17:28).

The thief (the devil) comes to steal (John 10:10). The devil brings about fear in subtle ways; he is sneaky in that way. The devil will whisper lies to you little by little until he has engrossed himself in your thinking, so much so that you begin to be overwhelmed by the spirit of fear. When fear takes root in your spirit, it infects every part of your life until you become a slave to fear. If you have been dealing with the spirit of fear, know that greater is He living in you than he that is in the world (1 John 4:4). Feed your faith with the truth of God's Word and watch every fear tormenting you starve to death. Give no life to fear. That means do not speak in fear, do not walk in fear, and do not allow yourself to be overcome by the spirit of fear.

Fear is a mindset, but so is faith. Make the spirit of fear bow down to the Word of God. When fear tries to creep in, start declaring the Word, say what God says in His Word about why we ought not to fear. God says, fear not because He is with you (Isaiah 41:10). God says, be strong and of good courage. He says He will never leave you nor forsake you (Deuteronomy 31:6). God says, let not your heart be troubled (John 14:1). God says, yea, though I walk through the valley of the shadow of death, to fear no evil because He is with you (Psalm 23).

Speak the Word over your issues, over your affliction, and over your thought-life. God's Word is medicine to the soul. God's Word is healing for your wounds. As you meditate on God's Word daily, His Word will heal every broken place in your life. God's Word has healing power for every issue you face in life. Jesus Christ is the cure— there is a Balm in Gilead, and the Balm is Jesus Christ! Hallelujah!

Study the Bible in the areas where you have weakness so that when the enemy attacks you, you already have your armor on, and you are ready to quench every fiery dart he throws at you. James 4:7 in the Amplified Version says, "...submit to the authority of God. Resist the devil [stand firm against him] and he will flee from you." You cannot stand firm against the enemy if you do not know the Word of God. You cannot stand firm against the enemy if you are not submitted to God. You cannot be submitted to God unless you are under His authority. God's authority is His Word, and His Word is His authority.

Consider this: a police officer possesses a badge, and even when he is not "on duty," his badge still has authority. Even when he is not in physical uniform, his badge is not devoid of authority. But if he does not display his badge at the proper time, it is of no use. A badge shows proof of identification. An officer cannot just say to an assailant, "Holt, police, you're under arrest!" especially when out of uniform. But when he pulls that badge out and declares his authority, when he shows proof of his identity, then we as civilians must submit to his authority. That is the same way the Word of God is. If you do not have on your armor (*your badge*) when the enemy, who is an assailant to God's people, attacks you, if you are not armed with the Word of God, declaring His Word with the authority given to you as His child, knowing who you are in Christ (*Your identity is found in Christ as His child*), how can you come against what is coming against you?

We must stay armed with the sword of the Spirit, which is the Word of God, at all times. The Bible tells us that the devil roams around like a roaring lion seeking whom he may devour. But when you are armed with the Word of God, and you are submitted and surrendered to the Lord Jesus Christ, it does not matter how the enemy attacks you. He cannot devour you, and he cannot devour the truth of God's Word because you are armed for the battle.

Our mind is the battlefield of the enemy. That is where Satan attacks. That is where he opposes God's people (and everyone, for that matter) in the mind. If the enemy can poison your mind, he can poison your life. Do not allow the devil to rob you of the abundant life Jesus Christ came for you to have. Allow your life to be led by Christ, and the devil will never gain a foothold over you because you are submitted to God, because you trust in God, because you trust in His Word, and you stand firm on His promises. You must be anchored in Christ. To be anchored is to be secured to a vessel, to cause to be fixed in place, unable to immobilize, to steady. That is what fear does; it immobilizes you little by little until it gains a hold over you, until it grips you so tight you feel like you cannot move, until it feels like you are going to suffocate because it won't turn you loose.

Fear is a stronghold—an area dominated or occupied by a major area of predominance. But stay afloat because the Lord is a Stronghold too, and you can go to Him for shelter during the attack. "The LORD *is* good, a stronghold in the day of trouble; And He knows those who trust in Him" (Nahum 1:7). Jesus Christ is our protection from the enemy. He is our Defense. No matter how hard the enemy comes against you, no matter how much he threatens you or attempts to torment you with his lies, hold onto Jesus! Stand in the Truth of God's Word. The Lord will not allow you to be overcome by the enemy; stand still! The enemy is defeated—today, tomorrow, and forevermore. The battle has already been won at the cross! Jesus paid it all for you and for me. Now, let's walk in the victory of our Lord Jesus Christ! You have authority through Him to be victorious in every battle. After all, the battle is not yours; it's the Lord's, so use the Word of God as your weapon and allow God's Word to fight for you. The Lord has never lost a battle, not one, and He never will. The Lord is always victorious!

For years in my life, I suffered with the spirit of fear. As I mentioned earlier, the enemy will whisper lies subtly. The enemy whispered lies into my ear so subtly that I did not even recognize that it was the devil lying to me. I did not understand the tactics of the enemy until I began to fellowship with God, until I began to study His Word and understand the demonic forces that were against me. I just thought I worried a lot, not realizing that there was a spirit sent from hell to steal, kill, and destroy my life. I suffered from terrible anxiety as a result of the fear in my life. The anxiety was so great at one point that I could barely function on a day-to-day basis. I was depressed, I felt hopeless, and I wanted to give up on life and die. I spent so many years living in fear. Fear robbed me of my joy and my peace. Even after I had given my life to Christ, I was still tormented by the spirit of fear. In fact, it got worse. After I surrendered my life to Christ, the enemy began attacking me on greater levels than he had before. I now know that I was dealing with spiritual warfare. There was a war going on in heaven, a war between good and evil, a war for my soul. The enemy could not stop me from accepting Jesus Christ as my personal Savior, but he was and is still relentless in trying to invade my life with the spirit of fear.

When I first surrendered my life to Christ—became born-again—I did not know who I was in Christ, but now that I know how fearfully and wonderfully made I am in Him, the enemy no longer has any power over me. Yes, the devil still attacks me; he attacks every child of God. That is his objective—to stop the purposes and plan of God. But instead of allowing him to gain power over me with fear, instead of cowering and fainting in my mind like before, I now fight back, using the Word of God as my weapon against him. Submission to the Father is how to put the enemy under your feet and keep him there. I submitted to God and continue to do so every day. I resist the devil by declaring God's Word right in the moment of attack, and therefore, the enemy has no choice but to flee from me.

You have to fight back against the devil, not with screaming and yelling and tears. That does nothing. The devil is not afraid of you, but he is afraid of the God in you. When you declare God's Word out loud, His Word moves on your behalf. Remember, God's Word is active (Hebrews 4:12). God's Word will do what He sent it to do (Isaiah 55:11). The enemy will not flee from you until you have first submitted to God. We must continue to submit to Him daily; it is not a one-time occurrence.

Luke 10:19 says, "Behold I give you the authority to trample on serpents and scorpions, and over all the power of the enemy, and nothing shall by any means hurt you." We have authority over the enemy through Christ! We have authority through Christ over the devil and all of his demons. When he attacks you, attack him back by the Word of God. Tell him, "Shut up, you're a liar and the father of lies; there is no truth in you. Get thee behind me, in the Name of Jesus!" Tell him, "Satan, the Blood of Jesus is against you, and you cannot cross this bloodline!" Tell him, "It is written and forever remains written, Satan, you have been defeated by the Blood of the Lamb." Tell him, "I belong to Jesus; you have no place in my life!"

Assert your God-given authority over that old lying serpent. The enemy is subject to the Word of God. Say what you need to say and praise the Lord Jesus for the victory. Do not allow the enemy to say anything back. Let him know who has the power, and it isn't him! Be bold in Christ! The devil cannot even touch a child of God unless he has the Lord's permission. Disobedience gives the enemy permission. Being outside of the will of God gives the enemy permission (being disobedient to God can lead us out of the will of God). Walking in fear gives him permission.

Stay in the peace of God, and allow His *love* to lead you. Perfect love casts out all fear. Ask God to show you how to perfect your love-walk and watch how the enemy scatters. Love is the barricade against the enemy. Barricade yourself in God's Word, walk in love toward all people, stay in faith, be obedient to the Lord, cling to Jesus, and the enemy will not gain access to you because you are sheltered under the shadow of the Most High!

The story of Job is a perfect example of how the enemy has no power to attack God's children unless the Lord first gives him permission to do so. Job lost his children and his property, but He still worshiped God. He did not blame God for his situation; He blessed the Name of the Lord—God is still good, no matter what you may go through. He still loves you, and He is still on the throne. Why should we be downtrodden when our Redeemer lives?! Yes, it hurts when going through hardship or adversity. Yes, it is painful when circumstances happen that we would not have chosen, but that's life. God is still God, no matter what circumstances or situations you face in this life. Just because you face uncomfortable or difficult times does not mean that you are outside of the will of God. Sometimes those trying times are to grow you or to teach you or to show you something for your good, not to harm you. The rain falls on the just and the unjust (Matthew 5:45). What the enemy meant for evil against you, God meant it for good (Genesis 50:20). That is how perfect our God is. That is how amazing He is. God will take what was meant to destroy your life and use it to bring you out, to deliver you, and set you in the place He predestined for you before the foundation of the world. "It is good for me that I have been afflicted..." (Psalm 119:71).

To be afflicted is to cause grievous physical or mental suffering. Affliction hurts, but so does a life apart from Christ. If I had not been afflicted in my mind like I was, I may not have turned to the Lord like I did. I may not have decided to surrender my life to Him and choose to worship Him and praise Him the way I do. I was a wounded person, but the Lord Jesus healed all of my wounds and made me whole in Him and in Him alone. It is a process. It is painful to go through, but I am grateful for it. I'm better because of it. I'm stronger because of it, and I am wiser because of the pain I endured. It is a continual process of yielding, submitting, and surrendering to the Lord daily.

Fear is the opposite of faith. We can walk in fear, or we can walk by faith, but we cannot do both. Fear brings about dread. Dread is a fearful anticipation of something. Have you ever dreaded something? To dread is to be in terror of, to fear intensely, to anticipate with alarm or reluctance. To dread is to be very afraid. We should have a fear of the Lord; that is to reverence God [a feeling of profound awe and respect, and act of showing respect]. Reverential fear is different than the spirit of fear because the Lord does not torment us or cause us to dread. He does not cause us to be afraid of anything or anyone. God's desire for us is to walk in love *because perfect love casts out all fear.* Remember: "There is no fear in love; but perfect love casts out fear, because fear involves torment. But he who that fears has not been made perfect in love" (1 John 4:18).

It is all about love. The reason why we are here on the planet is to have a relationship with the Father through His Son, Jesus Christ, and to be perfected in love. God is love, and love never fails. We cannot be perfected (lacking nothing essential to the whole, complete of its nature or kind) in love when we are perpetually flinching and fawning in fear. We have the divine nature of Christ (see 2 Peter 1:4). The Lord does not fear, and since His nature is in us, we do not have to fear either because God is in control. Fear is not the will of God. His will for all of us is love; loving Him with all our heart, with all our soul, with all our mind, and with all our strength, and loving our neighbor as ourselves (see Mark 12:28–31).

One of the names of God is Jehovah-Nissi, *The Lord Is My Banner* (Exodus 17:15). Any time that fear creeps in, remind yourself that the Lord is your Banner, and His banner over you is love. See how that coincides? God is love. His banner over us is love. There is no fear in love. Perfect love casts out all fear. The Lord is perfect in all His ways. We love God because He first loved us. God has always loved us because that is who He is! *GOD IS LOVE! Selah*—pause and think on that.

Overcoming fear is not a one-time event. It would be wonderful if we never experienced any kind of fear; however, that is unrealistic. Fear will always try to take root in our spirits, especially as a believer, but we do not have to allow it to grow. Remember, as I mentioned earlier, the place where the enemy attacks is in the mind. But we serve the God that sits high and looks low (Psalm 113:4–6). That means God has regard for us. He thinks of us. He considers us in a particular way. He looks at us attentively. He observes us closely. He is concerned for us. No one else loves us in that way except the Lord. No one loves us more than He does. What an honor and a privilege it is for you and for me to have such a loving, attentive, considerate, and merciful Father as our heavenly Father. There is no love greater than that.

We serve the One True Living God, Jesus the Christ. Our God is alive and well. He is Sovereign; He reigns, and He rules. He has all of us in His hands. Therefore, we have no reason to fear. Even when you feel fear, do not allow it to take root by meditating on the fear. Instead, meditate on God's Word; meditate on what the Lord says about you, and not what your emotions would have you believe. Roots have the potential to grow, but instead of allowing fear to take root, choose to be rooted and grounded in the Word of God, and fear will wither away and die because you refuse to give life to it. Fear is a thief sent from the pit of hell to destroy you. Fear is the opposite of faith. Cast all your cares on Jesus, for He cares for you (see 1 Peter 5:7). To cast is to throw with force, to let fall, drop, to turn.

Are there fears in your life that you need to cast onto the Lord? Do it today! Do not wait any longer. Start declaring the Word over your fears. God's Word is a weapon. The Name of the Lord Jesus Christ is mighty; His Name is above all names. Call on the Name of Jesus. When you are attacked by fear, take authority over it in Jesus' Name. Luke 10:17 tells us even the demons are subject to us in His Name—demons have to bow at the Name of Jesus. Demons tremble at the Name of Jesus. Cast all your cares on the Lord. You do not need to carry the burden of fear any longer. It was never your burden, to begin with.

Choose to live in the peace of God. You do not need to punish yourself any longer by living in fear. You are forgiven. The chastisement (punishment) of our peace was upon Jesus when He went to the cross (see Isaiah 53:5). Choose today to give your burdens to the Lord. Cast all your cares on God and leave them with Him. God can take care of you better than you can. He is our Protector, our Refuge, and our Shield. Find rest in His Word and let go of what has been weighing you down and keeping you bound. He promises to never leave you or forsake you. Trust Him.

## Pray this prayer:

*"Lord Jesus, I cast my cares on You, because You care for me. I cast every wrong thought, every fear, every anxiety, and every worry onto You. I release the weight of my cares to You, once and for all. I trust You to do what Your Word promises me. You are not a man that You should lie. What You have spoken in Your Word delivers me from every care that I have. I give them all to You. Thank You for taking my cares. Thank You for carrying my burdens so I don't have to. In Jesus' Name, I pray. Amen!"*

As long as we are in this earthly body, we will always be opposed by spirits of darkness. But thanks be to God who brought us out of darkness into His marvelous light (see 1 Peter 2:9). Thanks be to God who is merciful to us that He will not forsake us in our weaknesses. When the forces of darkness come against you, you can take refuge in the Lord; you can take refuge in His Word. You can run to Jesus for safety. He is our Strong Tower, the righteous run to Him and are safe (Proverbs 18:10).

Fear cannot overtake you if you do not allow it to. Whatever we meditate on will eventually take root (become firmly established, settled) in our lives. But when we allow the Word of God to be established in us, when we allow His Word to take root and be cultivated in us, we can remain confident that Jesus Christ has already settled it all.

Before Jesus gave up His Spirit to the Father on the cross, He said, "It is finished!" What's finished, you ask? That means that the Scripture has been fulfilled. That means that Jesus accomplished His God-given purpose in the earth (see John 19:28–30). The Word of God is settled with finality, and it cannot be undone. His Word cannot change; it does not need to change because it is already perfect. Change is only necessary when there is an insufficiency, and there is no insufficiency in God. He is sufficient. His grace is sufficient. It is by His grace that we can take refuge in Him. It is by His grace that we are saved. It is by His grace that we are not consumed. It is by His grace that we can call on the Name of Jesus and be shielded from all evil.

The next time fear attacks you, think on what is true, honest, just, pure, lovely, and things of good report.

Think on things that are praiseworthy (Philippians 4:8). Praise unto God breaks yokes. Praise unto God breaks strongholds. Praise unto God brings about deliverance. Praise unto God gets your mind off of you and focused on Him. So, instead of worrying, worship the Lord. Worship His Holy Name. Give Him glory, honor, and praise that the battle has already been won. Praise Him because He loves you, and He always watches over you. Guard your heart; the Lord will guard your life. Your life is not even your own; it belongs to the Father. He is God, the First and the Last, the Beginning and the End. He is the Ancient of Days. He knows your end from your beginning. Your story has already been written. You do not have to worry about anything; nada, zip, zilch! Turn it all over to the Lord. Have faith in God. Trust Him completely. Take Him at His Word and watch every fear fall to the ground. And remember, do not pick it up again; leave it in the Lord's hands and trust Him to deal with it as only He can.

CHAPTER FIVE

# Circumstances

Circumstances are events that occur beyond our human control. A loved one passes away unexpectedly, your company downsizes and terminates your employment, you receive an unfavorable medical report... Whatever the issue is, it is not an event that you would have chosen, but it happened nonetheless. It is not anything that you did wrong, but it happened anyway. You are not being punished by God; it's a circumstance. God's not mad at you and trying to make you suffer; it's a circumstance. Even in the most crushing times of life, God has a purpose—whether to grow your faith or to strengthen your relationship to the Lord or to teach you something. There is always purpose in pain. You would not have chosen it, but it happened. The question is, *how* can you grow from it? How can you seek God even in the midst of your pain? How can you depend on the Lord, even in times of grief? What is God's purpose in this pain? Remember, in Genesis 50:20, what was meant for evil against you, God meant for good.

Circumstances happen to all of us. Life is a series of

ups and downs, highs and lows, sorrows and joys, setbacks and comebacks, disappointments and successes. If God allowed it, He also purposed it. Everything that God allows to happen in your life is not to harm you or cause you to become morose or sullen. But there is purpose in it. Even in the darkest times of life, the Lord has a purpose. "... Weeping may endure for a night, But joy comes in the morning..." (Psalm 30:5)

The year was 1991. I was one month away from graduating from the 8th grade. Beyond excited for summer vacation, I looked forward to roller skating at the local roller rink, sleepovers with my best friend, and going to the community pool. My summer was going to be awesome, I thought, until an event that happened changed my life completely.

It was a typical Friday morning. I woke up at 6:30 a.m. to get ready for school. I showered, dressed, and fixed my hair in my signature ponytail. I got a Coca-Cola from the fridge and a bag of chips from the pantry. I could not wait to get to school that day. There were several exciting events that were due to take place in the coming weeks. But, there was one event that I never imagined would happen to me— an event that was life-altering.

I can remember it like it was yesterday. It was a beautiful spring day. I said goodbye to my mom and left the house. She usually saw me off to school before going to work. I took the same route as I did every day. My bus stop was just two streets over from my house. Up until that day, I did not have a care in the world. I was an innocent girl, so naive to the evilness of this world. I was full of life and joy. I was a child, and I behaved like a child. I was playful, joyful, and filled with zeal about life. I lived in a pretty little house with my parents, an only child. I had everything and anything my heart desired. But on that day, I lost something (for a little while) that I did not even know that I had: my security. I did not know that I had lost my security, but I had. To be secure is to be free from anxiety and worry. Back then, I had never heard of anxiety. But that was something that I would struggle with for years in my adult life.

As I walked to the school bus stop, I had a feeling in the pit of my stomach as if I was being watched. I did not hear anything, but I sensed it in my spirit. When I turned around, I saw a man in a blue van driving slowly behind me. At first, I thought he must be lost or looking for an address. But something did not feel right. I now know that it was the Holy Spirit Who was speaking to me, warning me that something was wrong. I began to walk faster; as soon as I did, the man drove away. I thought for sure that I was making something out of nothing, so I ignored that still, small voice and went on about my day. We all possess that still, small voice. Some call it intuition, but I now know that it is God. It is the Holy Spirit, Who is my Guide, Who lives on the inside of me as a believer in Christ.

When I returned home from school, I called my mom

at work to let her know I had made it home safely. I did not mention what happened that morning. I really did not think much about it at all. I went skating that Friday night with my friends as I did most Friday nights, I worked over that weekend at my part-time job, and I never even said a word to my parents; that is how innocent and naive I was.

The weekend came and went. That Monday, I left for school at my usual time. As soon as I left my house, there he was again. This time, he was parked on the side of my street. I felt a sense of alarm in my spirit. I then knew that something was definitely wrong. I ran back into the house, yelling for my mom. She was startled by me bursting through the door. I told her that there was a man sitting in a van and that he had followed me the Friday before. When my mom went to look out the window, the man drove away.

My mother questioned me as to why I had not told her about the man before. From the time I could remember, my mother had instilled in me to not keep secrets from her, to always tell her anything that bothered me, no matter how minuscule it may seem. She taught me on many occasions what to do if a stranger were to approach me or bother me in any way. She talked to me about being aware of my surroundings and always trusting that little voice inside. I apologized for not telling her sooner. I explained to her that I did not think it was a big deal. She assured me that it was not my fault.

A couple of months before this incident took place, I

started wearing lipstick. I loved how I looked when I wore lipstick; I felt like such a young lady. For a split second, I blamed myself. I could not understand that it was not anything that I had done wrong, but there was something wrong with the person who would ultimately stalk me for weeks. Parents, that is incredibly important to reassure your children that it is not anything that they did wrong. Do not ever blame your child for the actions of an adult. It is not how they look or how they dress or anything about their physical appearance to give anyone else permission to harm them.

After my mom talked with me, she called the police, and an officer came out right away. My mother and the officer stood in the foyer, talking about what had taken place. He spoke with me, and I gave him a description of the man and his vehicle. After that, my mother sent me to my bedroom until she was finished speaking with the officer. I pretended to go to my room, but I was eavesdropping from the kitchen. On the mantle were family pictures, including my school photos. I still remember the police officer's words. He said, "Your daughter is a very pretty little girl. That is probably what attracted the man. He most likely is a predator." *A predator*, I thought. I had no idea what that word meant. I went to my bedroom and looked up the word in the dictionary (reading the dictionary was something that I enjoyed doing). The meaning of the word was "a person who looks for other people in order to use, control, or harm them in some way." After reading that, my stomach had the most nauseating feeling. *Harm me?* I thought. *Harm me how?* My fourteen-year-old mind could not comprehend such heinousness.

For the next week, the police officer sat at the end of my street every morning, waiting to see if the man would show up again, but the man did not come around—not that week, anyway. I'm convinced that the man saw the officer monitoring my street, and that is why, for a little while, he left me alone. I was relieved.

My mom alerted the neighbors about the man. They watched out for me every day after that, but they could not watch everything; my neighbors could not protect me like the Lord can. A classmate who lived down the street began stopping by my house to walk to the bus stop with me every day until the end of that school year. He walked me home, too, every day from that time on. He would make jokes about "some creep," watching my every move. He did not mean any harm; he was just being a kid. But, deep down, I was scared. I began to have nightmares of the man taking me away and never being able to see my mom again. I was afraid to stay at home alone. I was constantly nervous. I was extremely distrustful of people after that.

After a week of surveillance by the police, they decided to let it go. My parents were told that if we needed anything or if the man showed back up again, to call them right away and to try and get the tag number so they could investigate further. The officer said the man probably gave up and moved on.

I thought it was over until the following week. As I was getting ready for school, I heard that still, small voice again; this time, I heeded the voice of God. The Holy Spirit told me to go out through the back door because, this time, if the man was there, I could see him through the fence before he could see me. I had never gone out through the back door before when leaving for school. We had a six-foot gate around the back of our house, where the backyard was. I could see through the slats from the inside, but it was not as easy for someone to see inside the gate from the outside. When I walked outside, I peered through the gate, and there he was again, but this time there was another man with him. The other man was in the passenger seat, with the seat lying back, as though he were hiding. I darted back inside the house, screaming the loudest scream I had ever screamed, crying out for my mom. My mother came running down the stairs in a panic. I knew we had to get his tag number. I knew we would not have another opportunity, so my mom and I jumped in the car. We ran out the front door since he was parked down at the back of the house. When he saw my mom, he sped off, but not before I was able to get the tag number. I was livid! I yelled at the man to leave me alone! He drove away so fast that his tires screeched down the street. My mother then called the police. When the police officer arrived at my house, my mother gave the officer the tag number and told him about the second man in the van.

The next day, the officer came to my house early in the morning. He talked with my parents and explained to them his findings. The man in the blue van was a convicted rapist. He had only been out of prison a short while. Officers brought him in for questioning the previous night. Since he had never approached me, there was not an actual crime that had taken place. Back then, anti-stalking laws did not exist. But, thank God, I never saw the man in the blue van again.

Always listen to that still, small voice; it is the Holy Spirit, Who dwells in those who believe on Him. The Lord protected me during this horrific time in my life. If I had not heeded the voice of God, I know I would not be here today. I believe in my heart that I would have been raped and killed by the men. But God blocked it! When the enemy came in like a flood, the Lord raised up a standard against him by His Spirit! Hallelujah! I thank the Lord for covering me. I thank the Lord for the Blood of Jesus that protects me. And I thank the Lord for always keeping me. He is a loving Father, Who is an all-powerful, all-knowing, and all-seeing God. He is Sovereign, and I am grateful to be His child.

It took me months to heal from that terrible ordeal. Most of that summer was spent inside. I was only allowed to go out when my parents were with me. I did not have any sleepovers with my best friend. I never went skating again. I could not go to the mall alone like before. I stopped working at my part-time job. I was miserable, but I was safe. I know my mom was only trying to protect me, but it really hurt me in ways I could not even explain at the time. I felt isolated. I felt alone, and as a result, my attitude changed for the worse. I became defensive, argumentative, and aggressive. I had it in my mind that I had to protect myself. The enemy had whispered so many lies to me that my young mind could not handle the constant attacks.

The Lord shielded me from being raped and killed, and I am so grateful that He covered me with the Blood of Jesus. God would not allow the devil to have his way. The enemy could not use someone to rape me, so he raped my mind over and over and over again. I walked in fear, and that was a gateway for him to attack me. I did not know the Word of God like I do now. I did not know I could call on the Name of Jesus and He would step in. I did not know the authority I had through Christ. I was a child, and I acted like a child. So, when the devil would attack me, I did not pray or call on the Name of Jesus; instead, I had tantrums. I acted out in my behavior by being mean to others. If I deemed someone as a threat, I would attack them before they could attack me. That is how warped my thinking was. My attitude was terrible. But thanks be to God who always leads us in triumph in Christ (see 2 Corinthians 2:14).

The following school year, I went to a youth prayer group with a friend. She invited me to her church, and I was excited to fellowship with other kids my age. I had been in church since I was a little girl, baptized when I was just five years old. Up until that point, the only prayers I prayed were my bedtime prayers and grace before meals. But on that day, something was changing on the inside. I did not recognize it at the time, but the Lord was beginning to do a work in me. I remember sitting in a circle with the other boys and girls, and the Youth Leader asked if anyone wanted to pray. So, I began to pray out loud. I had never prayed like that before, especially in front of anyone else. I do not remember exactly what I was praying about, but I do remember praying fervently; tears were streaming down my face. I do remember saying that my life is not in vain. When I opened my eyes, the other kids were looking at me as if I were from outer space. I was not concerned with what they thought of me. I knew the Lord had touched my heart at that moment. I did not fully understand what was happening, but I knew that God is real and that He loves me.

Even though we may go through circumstances in life that may try to hinder us or try to hinder our walk with the Lord, remember: God always has the final say. What God has blessed cannot be cursed. Hallelujah to the Lamb of God, for His love covers!

*Yes, Jesus loves me.*

*Yes, Jesus loves me.*

*Yes, Jesus loves me.*

*For the Bible tells me so!*

# CHAPTER SIX

# Faith in God

The Scripture tells us in Hebrews 11:6, "But without faith it is impossible to please Him, for he who comes to God must believe that He is and that He is a rewarder of those who diligently seek Him." To have faith is to have belief in God; it is a confident or unquestioning belief in the truth (Jesus is the Truth); it is a strong or unshakable belief in something, especially without proof or evidence. Hebrews 11:1 says, "...faith is the substance of things hoped for, the evidence of things not seen." I have not seen God in the natural, but I know that He is real. I know that He is alive and active. I know that He is the Creator of heaven and earth. I know that He is the One True Living God, and before Him, there was nothing. I believe with all my heart that the Lord Jesus Christ died for you and for me and that His love is constant in our lives, even when we do not see it, even when we do not feel it, even when we do not understand it; it is.

The Gospel of Christ is for all of us. "...it is the power of God to salvation for everyone who believes, for the

Jew first and also for the Greek" (Romans 1:16). He is God of all, Creator of heaven and earth, the First Cause of everything. Whether He is accepted by all or not, Jesus Christ is LORD! The Name of Jesus is above every name. The Father exalted Christ, a Man who knew no sin, became sin for us, and gave His life for us on the cross. And because Christ humbled Himself and became obedient to the point of death—even the death on the cross—God exalted Him and has given Him a Name above all names. The Lord Jesus is Sovereign; He reigns, and He rules. Every knee will bow, and every tongue will confess that Jesus Christ is Lord—believer or not (see Philippians 2:10).

All other gods are false; they do not exist. There is no Mother Nature. The Lord is the Creator of heaven and earth. He controls the seasons, the wind, and the rain… He created everything in the earth and under the earth. Buddha is not God. That is a statue created by man, a graven image, an idol. Muhammad is not God. He was a man who is dead and gone. There is no god of the sun or god of the moon or god of the stars; all of that is idolatry. Why worship the sun, moon, and stars? Why worship creation when we can worship the Creator? I do not have to see God in the flesh to believe in my heart that He is. When you have had a true encounter with the Lord Jesus Christ, you will believe that He is God and God alone. There is only One Savior, One Man who died for the sins of the whole world, One Redeemer who purchased all our liberties, Who bought us back from the hand of the enemy, One God who sits on the throne of grace, and His Name is Jesus the Christ, the Messiah, the Anointed One.

> *"You shall not have any other gods before Me. You shall not make for yourself a carved image—any likeness of anything that is in heaven above, or that is in the earth beneath, or that is in the water under the earth; you shall not bow down to them nor serve them. For I, the LORD your God, am a jealous God, visiting the iniquity of the fathers upon the children to the third and fourth generations of those who hate Me, but showing mercy to thousands, to those who love Me and keep My commandments."*
>
> **Exodus 2:3–6**

You cannot have true faith in God unless you first believe on the Name of Jesus Christ. The name *Jesus* means "God our Salvation." *Salvation* is the preservation or deliverance from destruction, difficulty, or evil. It is deliverance from the power of the penalty of sin. It is redemption. In Hebrew, His name is *Yeshua HaMashiach*, meaning "Jesus the Messiah." Messiah is the promised Deliverer of the Jewish nation.

> *"For He has rescued us and has drawn us to Himself from the dominion of darkness, and has transferred us to the kingdom of His beloved Son, in whom we have redemption [because of His sacrifice, resulting in] the forgiveness of our sins' penalty]. He*

*is the exact living image [the essential manifestation] of the unseen God [the visible representation of the invisible], the firstborn [the preeminent one, the sovereign, and the originator] of all creation. For by Him all things were created in heaven and on earth, [things] visible and invisible, whether thrones or dominions or rulers or authorities; all things were created and exist through Him [that is, by His activity] and for Him. And He Himself existed and is before all things, and in Him all things hold together. [He is the controlling, cohesive force of the universe.] He is also the head [the life-source and leader] of the body, the church; and He is the beginning, the firstborn from the dead, so that He Himself will occupy the first place [He will stand supreme and be preeminent] in everything."*

**Colossians 1:13–18 (AMP)**

Faith in God is vital in the life of every believer. Without faith, there is no true belief in God. Without faith, there is no trust in God. Every relationship is built on trust, even a relationship with our heavenly Father. If you do not trust Him, how can you be in relationship with Him? If there is no trust, there is no relationship. *Selah*—pause and think on that.

God gave His only begotten Son to all of humanity so that through Him we might be saved. Jesus Christ died on the cross; He went to hell and the grave so that we will not have to. Jesus paid our sin debt in full with His life. The Holy Spirit is in all places at once. God knows everything, and He knows everything about you. God sees everything, He sees you, and nothing is hidden from Him. God hears your prayers, your cries, and He knows your innermost thoughts and feelings. God removes your transgressions (sins) as far as the east is from the west, and He remembers them no more (Psalm 103:12). The Lord is compassionate (Psalm 103:13). All the characteristics of the Lord demonstrate how trustworthy He is. The Lord's goodness and mercy toward us, even in the midst of our ugliest moments, in spite of the many times that we fall short, He forgives us, and He loves us anyway; that's trustworthy. The Lord is not allowing you to be consumed by your sins, but instead, His mercy and His grace covered you when the enemy should have had his way and taken you out; that's trustworthy.

Reflect on all the times that the Lord kept you from harm and danger. Reflect on how His grace covered you when you were deep in sin. Reflect on all the times He protected you from yourself and the wrong decisions that could have cost you your life. Reflect on the people and situations that He prevented you from being part of. Reflect on how He loved you when you were unlovable. Reflect on how He remained faithful to you, even when you were unfaithful to Him, even when you turned your back on Him and cast Him aside. If all of that is not enough for you to trust the Lord…

God is better to us than we are to ourselves. He is an

awesome God, filled with love, joy, peace, long-suffering, kindness, goodness, faithfulness, gentleness, and self-control (see Galatians 5:22). He is altogether lovely. He is altogether wonderful. Our God is wonderful in all His ways. All of those attributes of God are more than enough to show you how trustworthy and faithful He is. There is no one like Him, and there never will be. He is the Alpha and the Omega, the Beginning and the End (Revelation 1:8).

You can have faith as small as a grain of mustard seed, and you can say to a mountain, "Move from here to there," and it will move, and nothing will be impossible for you (see Matthew 17:20). Moving mountains in your life is to move a considerable or serious difficulty; it is an obstruction that is difficult to overcome. We all have something in our lives that is an obstruction, something that attempts to keep us from accomplishing the purpose and plan of God for our lives, something that is difficult to overcome on our own. What in your life do you need to move? Is it fear? Is it anxiety? Is it doubt? Is it worry? Whatever your mountain is, speak to it in the Name of Jesus—tell it to move! Tell it to get out of your way! Cast it into the sea! Believe in your heart that it is moved. Do not doubt. Do not worry. Take God at His Word and watch every mountain in your life crumble and fall away.

Allow the Spirit of the Lord to move in your life. Allow His Holy Spirit to do in you what you can never do on your own. Let go of thinking that you can do "it" in your own strength; that is a deception of the enemy. Do not try and be independent of God. Depend on Him like a baby depends on their mother. When you rely on God, you will never be led astray. He will lead you in the paths of righteousness for His Name's sake. Call on His Name in the midst of your trouble. Call on His Name, whether happy or sad, in and out of season, in all circumstances. Call on the Name of Jesus always.

## Shout His Name right now—JESUS!

There is power in the Name of Jesus. Demons tremble at the Name of Jesus. Allow Jesus to be your strength; that means He is your Rock and your Fortress and your Deliverer, your God, your Strength, in whom you trust, your Shield and the Horn of your Salvation, your Stronghold (see Psalm 18:1–2). Take hold (grab onto Him and never let Him go)! Jesus is everything to those who believe. Have faith in God; He is always faithful to His Word. Declare the Word of God back to Him. When the enemy attacks you, attack him right back with the Word of God. Remember, even demons are subject to us in the Name of Jesus (Luke 10:17). That means you have authority over the enemy. Hallelujah!

The devil is after your faith. If he can rob you of your faith in God by causing you to doubt God, he can destroy your whole life; don't let him. Where there's doubt in God, there's doubt in His Word. But faith in God is faith in His Word, which are His promises. The Word of God is filled with promises from the Lord. He promises to never leave you nor forsake you (Deuteronomy 31:8). He promises to be our anchor (a source of security or stability) of the soul (Hebrews 6:19–20). He promises to be our help (Psalm 121:1–8; Psalm 54:4; Hebrews 13:6; John 14:26). Take your life back! Walk by faith and not by sight. Allow the Spirit of the Lord to lead you and direct your steps. The Lord will not allow the righteous to fall (Psalm 55:22).

As mentioned previously, Romans 10:17 tells us that "… faith comes by hearing, and hearing by the word of God." The more that you fill your heart and mind with the Word of God, the more your faith in God will grow. It takes time to grow in God. It takes time to grow in His Word and in the knowledge of Him. The Apostle Paul said, "The just shall live by faith" (Romans 1:17). What does it mean to live by faith? Living by faith is to have confidence in Christ. Faith in God is an unwavering belief that He is who He says He is in His Word. Faith is trust in God. When we live by faith, we trust in God, we hope in God, and we hope in His Word. To have faith is to have an unshakable belief that is not based on proof.

> *"Now faith is the substance of things hoped for, the evidence of things not seen."*
> **Hebrews 11:1**

The wonderful thing about the Lord is even when we do fall short, He offers the gift of repentance. He allows us another chance and another chance and another; that is how merciful the Father is. He is the God of forgiveness. When we confess our sins and repent, He removes our sin, He removes our pain, and He removes our shame; that is how faithful our God is. Even when we are faithless, God is still faithful (2 Timothy 2:13).

# CHAPTER SEVEN

## Disappointments

Disappointments happen to all of us. It happens to the just; the unjust; the rich; the poor; the famous; the unheard of; the preacher; the parishioner; the doctor; the orderly; the restaurant owner; the waitress; the governess; the housekeeper; the entrepreneur; the temp. Disappointments happen to everyone, including to me and to you. No one is exempt from becoming disappointed. Disappointment is a feeling of dissatisfaction that results when your expectations are not realized. It is a feeling of "letdown." We can build something up in our minds so much and expect a situation to be a certain way that when it does not turn out the way we hoped or expected, disappointment can easily set in.

A time in my life when I faced the greatest disappointment was during my now former marriage. I got married in my late twenties. Being married was something that I always wanted for myself. I wanted to be married to a wonderful man, have children, and live a "perfect" life. I wanted to drink coffee together, read the newspaper together, garden together, go out to romantic dinners, travel, and the list goes on and on. I had an idea of what I wanted, but what I wanted was a fantasy. I was more concerned with the wedding and the beautiful rings than the marriage and what the rings really symbolize: oneness, togetherness, a union, in good times and in bad. If I would have listened to the voice of God when He told me, "No, not yet," I would have saved myself a great deal of agony. I was constantly in a state of agony over my decision. I regretted it immensely. I would dwell on how I wished I had listened when my grandmother warned me against it. But I thought I knew best back then. I was dull of hearing the truth because I wanted what I wanted, and I did not take heed to godly wisdom from those who had my best interest in mind.

When things between my former spouse and me were good, I was happy, I was content. But when they were not, I wanted a divorce. I blamed my unhappiness on him when really I was unhappy with the choice I had made and thus unhappy within myself. I was more than willing to walk away and never look back again. Subconsciously, I wanted things to go wrong so that I would have an excuse to leave him and would not have to be riddled with the guilt of hurting him. There was no peace in our home because I was not at peace within myself. I would speak hurtful words. I would demean and ridicule him, and in turn, he would do the same to me. It was a vicious cycle. The words that my former spouse spoke to me were probably out of retaliation, but mine were what was in my heart. Out of the heart, the mouth speaks (Matthew 15:18).

I did not have a forgiving heart. If someone did me wrong, I would never speak to them again. I would discard a person with no problem at all. I was a grudge-holder, for sure. I allowed the spirit of resentment into my life by how I held onto what they "did" to me or how they treated me. Mistreat me, and that was it; there were no second chances with me. What a sad and miserable way to live, constantly holding onto hurts from the past. Thank God Jesus does not treat us in the same way. The Lord forgives us time and time and time again. He gives us more chances than we can count—that is how merciful our God is to us. The Lord is merciful even in times of disappointment. He is merciful even when we choose to go our own way and forsake His will. He is merciful even in our ignorance and our unwillingness to heed His voice. He is merciful even when we fall short of His glory and miss the mark. The Lord is full of mercy and grace, even when we mess up to the point where we "think" we cannot recover from our wrong decisions; His mercy endures.

I had a warped misconception that if I were to forgive someone for their wrongdoing, that would show me as weak, so, I wouldn't. But what makes us weak is when we do not forgive. What makes us weak is when we allow the hurt and pain of what someone "did" to us to override what Jesus has already done for us on the cross; He paid our sin debt in full.

Since the Lord forgives all our sins—past, present, and future sins—who are we not to forgive others in the same way? I know, it's easier said than done. But it can be done. You can forgive the people in your life who have hurt you and turn those hurts over to God and allow Him to heal your heart. You can allow the Lord to right the wrongs in your life and trust Him to deal with your enemies. All you need to do is cast your cares. Just because you forgive a person that does not mean that you set yourself up to be violated by them again.

A violation is a transgression or sin, a trespass. When someone trespasses against you, no matter how great that trespass is, find it in your heart to forgive them and let it go. You do not have to be in relationship with everyone; that is not what forgiveness is about. It does not mean that you have to break bread with them and allow them into your space, especially when you know they are not right for you or they are living a life contrary to godliness. But what it does mean is that in your heart, you have forgiven them and no longer hold them to what they "did."

The Lord is our Vindicator. He is our Defender. We cannot vindicate ourselves, only the Lord Jesus can do that, but we can free the people in our lives of their wrong-doings; even if they never apologize, we can free them because in freeing them, we are freed. Forgiveness is for you, not so much for them, but for you, so that you can move on with your life and be totally free from having an unforgiving heart. It may take many times to say, "Lord,

I forgive," but it can be done, and you can be totally free from the hurts and disappointments of your past.

"If we forgive people of their trespasses, our heavenly Father will also forgive us. But if we do not forgive people of their trespasses, neither will our heavenly Father forgive us of our trespasses" (Matthew 6:14–15). That is a sobering thought that when we hold onto hurt and offense and do not forgive people, the Lord will also not forgive us when we sin and do wrong.

Look back over your own life and recall a time when someone has wronged you in some way or betrayed your trust or offended you to the degree that you hardened your heart against that person or group of people; how does it make you feel when you think back on that hurt? Now, consider yourself. Consider the times that you did someone wrong or betrayed someone's trust or offended someone. Consider how that made the other person feel, consider how it hurt them or caused them emotional or maybe even physical pain. Consider how sorry you felt about the actions you committed against that person, how you wish you had never done what you did. Consider how they may have felt during that moment in time. Being able to look at yourself and considering your actions is sobering because it allows you to reflect on how your actions affected or impacted someone else in a negative way. Reflection allows you to examine your heart and make the necessary changes so as to do better the next time.

Holding onto unforgiveness is a trap of the enemy. Unforgiveness blocks the flow of God in our lives. When we live in a state of unforgiveness, we cannot hear clearly from the Lord. We can become spiritually deaf in a way. To live in a state of unforgiveness is to be in a condition or mode of being with regard to circumstances. When we allow the circumstances of what someone "did" to us to rule in our hearts and minds, we are, in a sense, bound to that hurt. It has a hold over us. When we constantly dwell on that hurt, eventually, it takes root and leads to bitterness. You can be free from the pain and hurt of your past when you allow Jesus to take your hurt and heal your heart.

## Say this prayer with me:

*"Heavenly Father, thank You that You alone carry my hurts and my pains. You alone carry the betrayals that I've endured. You alone carry my disappointments and any regrets that I have over my past. You saw every time that I've been hurt and wronged by the people in my life. You saw every tear that I've cried, and You put them in Your bottle and wrote them in Your book. Lord, because You forgive me time and time again, I too can forgive others. Because You do not hold my wrongdoings against me when I repent and turn from evil, I too let go of the wrongs committed against me by others. Even if they never apologize, I forgive them anyway. Even*

*if they are dead and buried, and they cannot ask me for forgiveness, I forgive them anyway. I no longer walk in unforgiveness. I no longer walk in bitterness and hold onto grudges. I release every disappointment, every betrayal, and every burden of bitterness to You. Cleanse my heart from all unrighteousness. Create in me a clean heart and renew a right spirit within me. Thank You for binding up my wounds. I receive Your healing by faith. And today, I choose to forgive. In Jesus' Name I pray, Amen."*

# CHAPTER EIGHT

## Weariness

The Scripture encourages us in Galatians 6:9 (KJV) to not be weary in well doing, for in due season we shall reap if we faint not. To be weary is to be physically or mentally tired. It is to be worn out, tired, or exhausted. Sometimes, when you have been doing the right thing for a long time or even for three months, and nothing seems to be happening or changing for the better, you can feel hopeless and give up. But I have come to realize that it is in those silent moments when nothing seems to be changing, when progress seems to be at a standstill, that is when the Lord is doing His greatest work in us. When it seems hard, and you want to give up and just say, "Forget it!" that is when you have to dig your heels in deeper and press forward, no matter how hard it is, no matter how you may feel, no matter what, keep going and do not quit. When you feel like giving up, that is when you are closest to your breakthrough.

I cannot tell you how many times in my life I have given up, how many times I have quit when the going got tough. Instead of hanging in there and pressing on, I fainted in my mind and said, "This is too hard. I don't want to do this anymore. It's not happening fast enough. Is this really worth it?" And the answer is, "Yes, it is worth it!" Trust the process. Everything is not going to just fall into your lap. Look at all of the men and women of faith that the Lord used in the Bible; none of them received what the Lord had for them without going through a process, and oftentimes it was a difficult process. It is easy to live in mediocrity, it is easy to live an average life just doing the average things, but it takes guts to be exceptional. It takes guts to live victoriously. It takes guts to accomplish your dreams. It takes guts to do what the Lord has called you to do and to be who He destined you to be.

Ever since childhood, when situations became too intense for me or I felt as though the task at hand was too difficult, I would quit. I would give up. I conceded because I thought I could not win, when the truth is, I really did not put forth the effort and try. I conceded to the opposition, the enemy. I allowed the devil to talk me out of my victory. I allowed the devil to lie to me and tell me how bad I was at something or how hard something was and how I wouldn't make it. Many times, I allowed the enemy to rob me of my potential. I allowed the devil to rob me of my aspirations and my goals because I believed his lies that I did not have what it takes to succeed, but the devil is a liar!

I am a perfectionist; it's a horrible trait because it brings about anxiety when something is not done how I deem it to be perfect or just so. For instance, when I write, I read the same passage of text over and over again to ensure that I have not made any mistakes in grammar, punctuation, etc. Editing your work is a good thing and should be done, but not to the extent that it causes anxiety and overthinking. Even after something is completed the way I like for it to be, I still mull over it and question whether I did it to the best of my ability. It is quite exhausting and can steal the joy in accomplishing tasks or goals. So, in turn, I often procrastinate. Procrastination is a thief. Say that with me: PROCRASTINATION is a thief. I have found myself often daydreaming about doing something, but when it came down to actually doing it, I would put it off. But know this, anything that the Lord puts in your heart to do, He also gives you the grace to accomplish it. The Lord will work in you and with you when you put forth the effort and work at it. What is your "it"? What is it that you have put off for far too long? What is it that the Lord has placed in your heart to accomplish, but you have put off for fear of failure? Let the fear of failure go today. Ask the Holy Spirit to help you in that area of weakness. Ask the Holy Spirit to show you how to accomplish your dreams without hesitation and without fear. Even if you feel afraid, do it anyway. Shame the devil by trusting God and trusting the purposes and plan of God for your life. This is the only life you will have in this world. Do not waste it by wondering what you could be; be it! What is the worst thing that could happen if you fail? So what, try again! If you are told no one hundred times, try one hundred and one times. Eventually, you will get the yes you have been believing God for. When the

Lord gets ready to open a door for you, no man will be able to shut it. Jesus says, "See, I have set before you an open door, and no one can shut it…" (Revelation 3:8).

Weariness is a feeling of being worn out—to be physically or mentally tired. It is to feel an overwhelming sense of fatigue, which is not remedied by sleep or rest. Weariness is a spirit. When a person is spiritually weary, there is a lack of strength to move forward. Weariness brings about a feeling of being stuck. To be stuck is to be trapped, caught, and ensnared. The enemy ensnares God's people, and the way he ensnares is with lies. Think of it this way—to be ensnared is to be set up, to be framed, or to be entrapped.

I'm sure you have watched on television or heard on the news about people who were sentenced to prison for committing a crime, only to be discovered years later to be found innocent and exonerated of that crime. All manner of ensnarement begins with a lie. When a person is framed or set up, a lie has been told, evidence may have been planted, words may have been twisted to suit the person handling the interrogation of a suspect, or a witness may have been coerced into lying or threatened in some way, but the evidence presented was actually false or tampered with in some way. A person could be falsely accused of a crime they had nothing to do with. That is what the enemy does. He is an accuser; he is a liar; he is a manipulator. The Bible says that Satan is an accuser of the brethren (Revelation 12:10).

In Matthew 22:15, the Pharisees (who Jesus called hypocrites) attempted to trap Him by distorting what He said. But Jesus knew their intentions, and He did not fall prey to their deception. Jesus was not ignorant of their devices (attitude of mind, especially one that favors one alternative over others). That is the way we as believers have to be. We are not ignorant of the devices (schemes) of the devil (2 Corinthians 2:11). If we are aware of Satan's devices, if we know what tactics he uses against us, we have an advantage over him, not the other way around. Some of the devices or schemes that the devil uses are fear, worry, doubt, unbelief, reasoning, rejection, offense, isolation, hopelessness, and so on. It all starts with a thought. When the enemy sets out to ensnare or entrap us, he does so by planting thoughts of deception. Once he is able to deceive us, he begins to build up strongholds. A stronghold does not happen overnight. A stronghold of the mind is a lie that Satan builds up gradually. It is subtle. It is not immediately obvious. It is cunning—everything that the enemy does is wicked and for our harm, never for our good. The enemy does not warn; he threatens, he torments, he deceives, and he manipulates our perception.

Strongholds begin to take root when we believe the lies of Satan instead of trusting in what we know God says in His Word. Strongholds are magnified in our lives when we focus on the problem instead of the Problem-Solver, which is Jesus. Strongholds create a feeling of weariness because it is draining to the mind and sometimes to the body. It is draining to constantly be in a state of unrest and uneasiness. Any time you have a thought, and it does not line up with the Word of God, you can rest assured that the thought is false. And if it is false, it is not of God. The Lord never plants thoughts of wickedness in our minds. The Lord never utters a lie. The Lord never speaks of evil against you or someone else. Those are all deceptions of the devil. So when the enemy comes against your mind with these subtle thoughts, speak the Word against it; plead the Blood of Jesus over your mind and over your emotions. Believe God no matter what. The Lord does not change. His Word does not change. He does not threaten or intimidate us to make us fearful. The Lord will warn you of a situation to protect you, but it is up to you to listen and heed His warnings. The Holy Spirit will nudge you and tell you, "No, don't do that; that is not right for you; turn the other way." That is how much He loves us. The Lord's plan for our life is always for good, never for evil. He wants the best for us; that's love.

There have been numerous times in my life when I became weary. There have been numerous times in my life when I fainted in my mind when I felt hopeless and did not see how my situation would change. Even as a believer, I suffered from weariness. I would do the right thing for a while, and then a situation would happen, as it does in life, and I would give up and quit. I allowed weariness to supersede what Jesus already did on the cross. I allowed weariness to take control of my thinking. I allowed weariness to temporarily negate the promises of God in my life. I allowed weariness to wear me down. But just when I thought I could not feel any lower, Jesus stepped in and picked me up. Jesus stepped in and ministered to me by His Word. Jesus stepped in and loved me even at my lowest.

We serve a mighty God. We serve a loving Father. We serve the God of love. Jesus Christ is lovely in all His ways. He is full of grace and mercy. He is full of compassion for us. He knows what it is like to be tempted; He knows what it is like to suffer weariness. Remember when Jesus was in the Garden of Gethsemane? He prayed three times to the Father to take the bitter cup from Him because He was soon to be crucified. But after that, He said, "Not my will, but thy will be done." When we say, "Lord, not my will but Your will be done," that changes our whole perspective, that changes our outlook on how we see a situation. We can trust in the Lord, knowing that He will see us through every circumstance and every situation we face in life. Just because we are saved by grace does not mean we will not face difficulties and setbacks in life. But if we keep our mind on Jesus and continue to trust in Him, we can face those challenges of life with a heart of hope and blessed assurance because we know that God is with us and He is always fighting for us. He is with us in the storm, in the brokenness, and in the grief; the Lord is always near.

The key to overcoming weariness is to keep your heart and mind stayed on Jesus. Allow the peace of God to rule in your heart, not how you feel, not what you think, but what God says. Look to Jesus and remember how He was opposed on every side as He went to the cross. Remember how He was subjected to sinful men when He endured the cross. He could have come down off the cross if He wanted to. He could have called legions of angels to Him (Matthew 26:53), but He was obedient to the Father and endured the cross nevertheless. He gave His life for us. His life was not taken; He gave it so that we can be saved and called children of the Most High God. He gave His life so that we may live again in heaven with Him one day. He gave His life so that we can have life and life abundantly. So, the next time you begin to feel weary and faint in your mind, look to Jesus, the Author and Finisher of our faith (Hebrews 12:2), and remember how He suffered for you and did not lose heart, but He stayed nailed to that *old rugged cross* so that the Scriptures would be fulfilled and the Father's will be done.

If Jesus had grown weary and fainted in His mind during that time in His life, where would we be? Think on that the next time weariness tries to take hold of you and make you lose heart (become discouraged). You do not have to allow discouragement to set in because Jesus Christ is still on the throne. The Lord Jesus is alive and well. The Lord Jesus is capable of caring for you. He's got the whole world in His hands, and that includes you. He reigns, and He rules for all of eternity. Chin up! You are loved tremendously by the Lord, and love never fails but always prevails. Christ always prevails. The Lord is victorious, and through Christ, we are victorious too.

*"Finally, my brethren, be strong in the Lord and in the power of His might. Put on the whole armor of God, that you may be able to stand against the wiles of the devil. For we do not wrestle against flesh and blood, but against principalities, against powers, against the rulers of the darkness of this age, against spiritual hosts of wickedness in the heavenly places. Therefore take up the whole armor of God, that you may be able to withstand in the evil day, having done all, to stand, Stand therefore, having girded your waist with truth, having put on the breastplate of righteousness, and having shod your feet with the preparation of the gospel of peace; above all, taking the shield of faith with which you will be able to quench all the fiery darts of the wicked one. And take the helmet of salvation, and the sword of the Spirit, which is the word of God; praying always with all prayer and supplication in the Spirit, being watchful to this end with all perseverance and supplication for all the saints..."*

**Ephesians 6:10–18**

CHAPTER NINE

# Prayer

Prayer is a reverent petition made to God. Prayer is communion with God. It is a fervent request. Prayer is supplication. Supplication is to ask humbly or earnestly, as by praying. Prayer is thanksgiving to the Lord. When we pray, we give thanks to Jesus. When we pray, we humble ourselves under the Lord's mighty hand. When we pray, we seek the Lord's will and the mind of Christ. When we pray, we inquire of the Lord to find out what He thinks about "it." When we pray, we cast our cares on God. When we pray, we are comforted by knowing that God hears us and He knows what we need, even before we ask; God already knows. When we pray, we look to the Lord for direction. Prayer is important in the life of the believer. Without prayer, how can we go about our day in confidence? Without prayer, how can we be changed by the power of the Holy Spirit? Without prayer, how can we have any kind of security? Prayer is vital in the life of the believer—it is life-giving, life-saving, and life-changing.

We ought to pray first thing when we wake up. When

you wake up in the morning for work or for school or to get the children up to go to school before you begin your day, prayer should be your first plan of action. When you begin your day with prayer before the Lord, prayer directs the course of your day. When you get on your knees and worship the Father in prayer and thank Him for His faithfulness, for His grace, and His mercy, those prayers will lead you and guide you into all truth by the power of the Holy Spirit. Prayer will grant you the wisdom and discernment needed for the day. Prayer is surrendering to the Lord Jesus; it is admitting that you do not know what is best; it is saying to Jesus that you do not have it altogether; it is telling the Lord that you need guidance and counsel from Him. Prayer is a weapon against the evil one and his lies. Prayer is adoration to the Lord. Prayer is praise to the Lord. Without prayer, there is no relationship with the Lord. You cannot be in relationship with someone who you do not talk to.

Matthew 6:7 reminds us that when we pray, do not use vain repetitions as the heathen do. For they think that they will be heard for their many words. Therefore do not be like them. For your Father knows the things you have need of before you ask Him. In this manner, therefore, pray:

## The Lord's Prayer

*"Our Father which art in heaven, Hallowed*
*be thy name. Thy kingdom come. Thy will*

*be done in earth, as it is in heaven. Give us this day our daily bread. And forgive us our debts, as we forgive our debtors. And lead us not into temptation, but deliver us from evil: For thine is the kingdom, and the power, and the glory, for ever. Amen."*

**Matthew 6:9–13 (KJV)**

In Luke 11:1, Jesus was praying in a certain place, and when He was finished, one of His disciples asked Him to teach them how to pray as John also taught his disciples. *The Lord's Prayer* is the prayer that Jesus taught them.

When you pray, what is the motivation behind your prayers? Do you pray because you revere the Lord and want to honor Him in prayer? Do you pray out of fear of what could happen if you don't? Do you pray because there is some guilt or shame that you are not certain you have been forgiven for? Do you pray because you are trying to get God to do something? Do you pray because you think it will get you into heaven? Or do you pray because you need the Lord in every circumstance and every situation in life? Ask yourself those questions and be honest with yourself in your response. The Lord already knows your heart, He knows your agenda, and He knows your intentions. The question is, do you? *Selah*—pause and think on that.

Prayer has to be intentional; it has to be deliberate. That means you have to make it a priority to spend time with the Father in prayer. We pray when we wake up from a night's sleep. We pray before we go to sleep for the night. But the

Scripture encourages us in 1 Thessalonians 5:16–18 to pray without ceasing, to give thanks in all circumstances, not for all circumstances, but in all circumstances. That means, no matter what you may be going through, you can thank God that He is with you. You can thank God for His unfailing love. You can thank Him for His presence even in the midst of hardship and trials. Praying without ceasing is to pray to the Lord in every situation, no matter the circumstances. Praying without ceasing is to be persistent in prayer. Prayer does not have to be eloquent, using articulate words; it is just a conversation between you and the Lord. You talk to Him; He listens. He talks to you; you listen. It is communion.

The Lord speaks through His Word. You may pray about something, and then five minutes later or five hours later or five days later, the Lord will respond to your prayer by His Word. Be it in the written Word or by watching or listening to a ministry program or through someone in our lives—God speaks. He gives confirmation by His Word. It is about opening yourself up to hear what the Lord wants to say to you.

I remember a time when I was really struggling with fear and anxiety. I was constantly worried about germs and blood and keeping my children safe from harm. (When I became a parent, that is when fear and anxiety became a stronghold in my life, I was constantly worried about keeping them safe. I believe that stemmed from being stalked by a stranger in my childhood; I had an irrational fear of them being hurt.) As I was doing laundry, the Holy

Spirit said to me so quietly but distinctly, "The enemy uses blood against you, use the Blood against him." After that, I began to study scriptures on the Blood of Jesus. I began to appropriate (to set apart for specific use) the Blood of Jesus in my life, over my children, over my mind, over my coming and going, over my family. I pled the Blood constantly and still do because the Blood of Jesus is what redeemed us.

The Blood covers. The Blood leads. The Blood of Jesus saves, delivers, redeems, and sets the bondservant free. I was a slave to fear. Fear dominated my life, day in and day out, but the Blood of Jesus spoke for me and overruled the guilt and the shame of my past. The Blood of Jesus freed me from the bondage I was in. I no longer felt unworthy of God's love. That is what fear does; it lies and reminds you of your past to keep you from accepting the love of Christ. You may know God loves you because His Word says He does, but truly accepting His love in your heart requires trust.

When we trust God enough to tell Him our deepest thoughts and fears and cares and admit our weaknesses to Him in prayer, there is such freedom in that. Relinquishing those thoughts and cares to the Lord says to God, "I know You can handle this, so I'll leave it in Your hands. I trust You to deal with the issues of my heart. I trust You to do a work in me so that I can live totally free, without fear of what the devil threatens me with." That kind of faith lets God know that you know that He has your back in every situation, no matter the circumstance. You can talk to the Lord about anything, and He will see you through it.

> *"I love the LORD because he hears my voice and my prayer for mercy. Because he bends down to listen, I will pray as long as I have breath! Death wrapped its ropes around me; the terrors of the grave overtook me. I saw only trouble and sorrow. Then I called on the name of the LORD: "Please LORD, save me!" How kind the LORD is! How good he is! So merciful, this God of ours! The LORD protects those of childlike faith; I was facing death, and he saved me. Let my soul be at rest again, for the LORD has been good to me. He has saved me from death, my eyes from tears, my feet from stumbling. And so I walk in the LORD's presence as I live here on earth! I believed in you, so I said, I am deeply troubled, LORD." In my anxiety I cried out to you..." (vv. 12–14). "What can I offer the LORD for all he has done for me? I will lift up the cup of salvation and praise the LORD's name for saving me. I will keep my promises to the LORD in the presence of all his people" (vv. 16–19). "O LORD, I am your servant; yes, I am your servant, born into your household; you have freed me from chains. I will offer you a sacrifice of thanksgiving and call on the name of the LORD. I will fulfill my vows to the LORD in the presence of all his people—in the house of the LORD in the*

*heart of Jerusalem. Praise the LORD!"*

**Psalm 116:1–11, 12–14, 16–19 (NLT)**

Prayer does not change God. He does not need to change because He is already perfect. Prayer changes you. It changes your mindset, it changes your heart, and it changes your perspective. Prayer to God gives confidence because you trust that no matter what the response is from the Lord, the outcome is in your favor. Even if the answer is no, it is in your favor and for your good. Prayer to the Lord gives hope that *"this too shall pass."* Prayer says to God, "Lord, I trust You to take my burdens and deal with them in Your way and in Your timing." Prayer is not meaningless. Pray is meaningful to the Lord, and as a true believer in the Lord Jesus Christ, prayer must be a meaningful part of your daily life. Without prayer to God, there is no relationship with God, and consequently, there is no fellowship with Him either.

# CHAPTER TEN

# Deliverance and Healing

Prayer led me to seek professional counseling. For a little over a year, I saw a licensed therapist. She was a woman of God, which I did not know when I initially started seeing her. But from the first visit, I knew she was a godly woman. She was around the same age as my grandmother (who had passed away some years before that time). I saw her twice a week to start, and then as time went on, I would have once-a-week therapy sessions with her. Even though I knew from my time with her that she was a godly woman, it took me a long while to be able to trust her with my issues and my emotions. But eventually, the walls began to come down, little by little.

The one thing about therapy is that you have to be honest; that is the only way to true healing—to be honest with not only your therapist but with yourself as well. You cannot change what you will not confront. And I had many demons to confront. I had a demon of unforgiveness. I had a demon of anger. I had a demon of bitterness. I had a demon of fear. I had a demon of wrong-thinking. I had a demon of murmuring and complaining. I had a demon of guilt and shame and condemnation. I lived in the past. I wanted to change my past, but I couldn't. It was already done. But during my time in therapy, I learned that I could move forward and forgive myself for my sins because Jesus had already forgiven me when I confessed my sins to Him in prayer.

During one of my sessions, I was telling the therapist about a person who had hurt me and how I disliked this person immensely and how terrible of a person I thought they were and how much I wanted to pay them back for how they treated me. And she said to me in the kindest, most nurturing, and sweetest voice, "Nikki, have you ever thought of praying for them?" I was filled with such anger and resentment; I looked her right in her face and said, "No, why would I pray for them? I can't stand them." She then replied, "That's why you should pray for them so that you can forgive them and forgive yourself for the hostility you feel toward them."

I was so angry that I could not fathom praying for my enemy. I had such hatred in my heart toward them that praying for them was not something I ever thought I could do until one day… I did. It was not instant, but the more the Lord brought it to my attention, the more the Lord showed me how He forgave me for all of my ugliness and all of my evil ways and the wicked things that I have done and said about other people, the more my heart began to change toward that person, and I began to pray for them. I prayed that the Lord would change my heart toward them and show them loving kindness and mercy, just as Jesus shows me. I prayed that the Lord would bless them and keep them. I prayed for their well-being. I prayed that they would trust in and accept the Lord Jesus as their personal Savior. The more that I would pray for them, the more my heart changed. The more that I would pray for them, the less I dwelled on what they did. Instead, I focused my attention on the Lord and what Christ already did on the cross, how He is so gracious toward us, even when we do not deserve it. The more I focused on how Jesus died for the sins of the whole world—and not just mine, but for theirs too—the more those negative feelings about them began to dissipate.

Prayer to the Father will not always change the situation you are in, but it will change you. When we keep our hearts open to the love of Jesus, He can then open our hearts to loving those around us, even those who we deem unworthy of our love. Love is not always a feeling but a conscious decision. Just like unforgiveness is a decision, love is a decision. I would rather make the decision to walk in love than to walk in bitterness. Bitterness eats away at you; it is detrimental to your health; it limits your walk with God; it decreases your relationship with Jesus because it takes away *from*, instead of adding *to*. But when you walk in love, you can only increase: increase in joy, increase in peace, increase in faith, and increase in your relationship to the Lord.

The Scripture encourages us in 1 Thessalonians 3:12, "And may the Lord make you increase and abound in love to one another and to all, just as we do to you, so that He may establish your hearts blameless in holiness before our God and Father at the coming of our Lord Jesus Christ with all His saints." Walking in healing requires walking in love. When you are truly walking in healing, it shows in your interaction with others.

Have you heard the saying *"Hurt people hurt people"*? Show me someone who has a negative attitude, someone who is critical of others, someone who rarely has anything good to say about situations and especially about other people, or someone who is a chronic fault-finder and beneath that is an incredibly hurt person. None of us are exempt from experiencing hurt in life, some more than others, and everyone's hurt is different, but the cure for any and all hurt is Jesus Christ. We can take those hurts to Jesus in prayer and allow Him to heal our brokenness.

Brokenness is an event or a series of events in life that make one feel hopeless and in a place of despair. It is temporary. But when you trust in the Lord to heal the broken places in your life and do the work necessary to walk in divine healing, you will find that the brokenness that you went through was actually a blessing (Psalm 119:71). Affliction is a cause of great suffering. Whether it be mental or physical affliction, it hurts. It is heart-wrenching. It is stressful, and it can cause devastating depression. Affliction is oftentimes isolating, and it can be grievous. But there is hope. *"...constantly rejoicing in hope [because of our confidence in Christ], steadfast and patient in distress, devoted to prayer [continually seeking wisdom, guidance, and strength]"* (Romans 12:12).

Healing and prayer are connected. James 5:13, 14, 16 in the Amplified Bible says, "Is anyone among you suffering? He must pray..." Verse 14 of the text reads, "Is anyone among you sick? He must call for the elders (spiritual leaders) of the church, and they are to pray over him, anointing him with oil in the name of the Lord; and the prayer of faith will restore the one who is sick, and the Lord will raise him up..." Verse 16 goes on to say, "...and pray for one another, that you may be healed and restored."

Whatever has been ailing you, whether it is a physical ailment or an emotional (mental) ailment, you can pray to the Lord to be made well, to be healed of that affliction. To be healed is to restore to health or soundness; to set right; to repair; to recover from an illness or injury; to return to health; to experience relief from emotional distress.

The story in the Bible about the woman with the issue of blood is a great example of how healing and prayer are connected. She said to herself, "If I only touch His outer robe, I will be healed." Notice that the woman said to herself first, before she was actually healed, by touching the outer robe (hem) of Jesus' garment. Not only is that a great example of healing and prayer, but it is also a great example of faith and perseverance. Her faith in Jesus' ability to heal her issue made her well. But she said it within herself first, which in essence, she prayed before her healing was made manifest.

We all need to be healed of something. There are hurt people all around us. And just because they may smile and not talk about it does not mean that they do not have something in their lives where there is unresolved hurt and pain that keeps them stuck and in a place of bondage. If the woman with the issue of blood had not pressed her way through the crowd to get to Jesus, her affliction might have killed her. Just imagine the great suffering that this woman endured for twelve long years. Just imagine how she felt on a day-to-day basis, bleeding from her uterus. Imagine the embarrassment she felt not being able to go out in public because she was bleeding from her womb.

In those times (and maybe even still today in Orthodox Judaism), Jewish women were not permitted to go out in public during menstruation; they were deemed ceremonially unclean for seven days. Anyone who touched her during that time would also be deemed ceremonially (relating to the performance of a procedure) unclean until evening. If a woman had a flow of blood for many days that is unrelated to her menstrual period or if the bleeding continues beyond the normal period, she is deemed ceremonially unclean. Women were deemed unclean as long as the discharge continued.

Just imagine how isolated she must have felt. Imagine

her weariness from suffering with that condition for all those years. Surely she must have had an odor from bleeding for twelve years without any relief. Imagine the shame she must have felt dealing with that affliction. Imagine how exhausted she must have been. She had gone to many physicians, she had spent all of her money trying to get well, but then one day, she heard about a man named Jesus coming to her town. A man named Jesus, Who heals the sick and casts out demons. A man named Jesus, Who had the cure she needed so desperately that she risked the shame of the townspeople, who probably smelled her stench as she walked by and probably whispered about her and pointed at her as she pressed her way through the crowd to obtain her healing. But nevertheless, she pressed...

That is what I think about when studying the scripture about the woman with the issue of blood. The woman did not care about the possible consequences she could face for breaking the Law. She desired to be healed so desperately that she took the risk anyway. That kind of faith is bold. That kind of faith is what we need to have in this day and time, a bold, tenacious faith that cannot be halted, a bold faith that could end up costing you everything, but without it, losing everything anyway. *Selah*—pause and think on that.

# CHAPTER ELEVEN

# *Loss*

Loss is something none of us want to endure. When we lose something or someone, there is a sense of grief. Sometimes, there is a feeling of regret or a deep longing to regain what we once had. We can lose many things throughout our lifetime. Sometimes, there is a physical loss. Other losses are spiritual. We can lose our peace. We can lose our joy. There are even times when we can lose our faith in God (if only for a short while). Loss happens to everyone. A physical loss is inevitable. We will all lose loved ones along the way; that is part of life. But what about when we lose our confidence in God? It is not that the Lord has failed us in some type of way because God never fails. He is victorious in every circumstance of life.

When we lose our confidence in God, there is an issue within ourselves. How can I lose my confidence in God, you ask? Yielding to fear is one way to lose confidence in God. When we allow fear to rule in our lives, that opens the door to doubt. Doubt says that what God promises in His Word will not work, or maybe it just will not work for us.

Unresolved sin from the past can bring about doubt in the mind because there is a feeling that God has not forgiven you for something somewhere along the way. Even if you have repented of sin and turned away from it, there could still be a sense of loss because even if you believe in your heart that God forgave you when you repented, you may not have forgiven yourself.

Holding onto what you have lost and having a longing in your heart for what was lost can make you doubt the promises of God because you do not believe you are worthy of forgiveness. Feeling unworthy of forgiveness keeps one in condemnation. Condemnation always looks at the past; it cannot move forward. Condemnation keeps one stuck, and being stuck reminds one of what was lost.

You cannot move forward in God until you let go of the past. That means letting go of what you wanted, letting go of what did not work out the way you had hoped. That means letting go of hurt, letting go of bitterness, and letting go of what was. Paul said in Philippians 3:13, "...forgetting those things which are behind and reaching forward to those things which are ahead..." First John 1:9 encourages us, "If we confess our sins, He is faithful and just to forgive us our sins and to cleanse us from all unrighteousness."

The Lord is faithful and just to forgive us of our sins when we confess our sins to Him. We are forgiven. Jesus always forgives when we confess our sins to Him and repent of our wrongs. But what about when you have not been able to forgive yourself yet? There is a great sense of loss within us when we have not yet forgiven ourselves. I implore you today to forgive yourself. Forgive your failures. Forgive your wrong decisions. Forgive yourself for all the times you missed the mark and went your own way. Forgive yourself today so you can truly move forward in your walk with the Lord.

You are forgiven for past, present, and future sins. You have been justified by faith in Christ when you believe in and trust in Him and acknowledge Jesus as God's Son. You are declared free of the guilt of sin, made acceptable to God, and granted eternal life as a gift by His precious, undeserved grace through the redemption by His blood, which is provided in Christ Jesus. Jesus Christ is our atonement and reconciliation (propitiation). It is by His blood to be received through faith. This is to demonstrate His righteousness, which demands punishment for sin, because, in His deliberate restraint, God passed over the sins previously committed before Jesus' crucifixion (see Romans 3:21).

## Say this prayer with me:

*"Heavenly Father, thank You for Your forgiveness in my life. I receive Your forgiveness by faith. All the times that I messed up and went my own way, You have forgiven me. All the times I sinned against You and crucified You over and over again due to my*

*disobedience, You have forgiven me. You are merciful and gracious to me, slow to anger, and plenteous in mercy. Thank You for Your long-suffering toward me. Help me, Lord, to forgive myself for my wrong decisions. Help me to forgive myself for the way I lived in the past. Lord, Your Word says that You remove our transgressions from us as far as the east is from the west; that's how merciful You are toward us. So today, I choose to forgive myself. I give my failures to You, Lord, and believe in my heart that You are restoring unto me all that was lost, even what was lost due to my own willful disobedience to You, You are restoring me. I am forgiven. I am loved, and I am free from all guilt and shame. In Jesus' Name, Amen."*

If you will stand in faith that the Lord Jesus will restore to you all that was lost, you will finally be able to move forward as the Lord commanded, "forgetting those things which are behind and reaching forward to those things which are ahead..." (Philippians 3:13). You cannot stay stuck in what was. You must move forward in what is to come. There is more in store for you in God. There are battles to be fought in prayer, victories to be won by faith, and a calling on your life to be walked out and lived. You are called for the higher calling in Christ Jesus to defeat every enemy, every giant, and every hindrance that has come against the purposes and plan of God for your life. Greater is He! (1 John 4:4) Hallelujah!

You have to have a made-up mind that you will fight the good fight of faith. You have to have a made-up mind that you will accomplish the will of God. You have to have a made-up mind that Christ in you, the Hope of Glory, will be uplifted and glorified in your life. You have to have a made-up mind that you will stick with the Lord Jesus Christ, no matter the adversity; you will not quit; you will not concede to the enemy; you will not faint; you will not grow weary in well-doing; you will not throw in the towel, but you will stand and see the salvation of the LORD! You will go on. You will move forward. You will run the race that the Lord has set before you. You will run on to see what the end will be! You will go all the way with God! You will win because victory belongs to Jesus! Stay close to the Lord. Choose Him above anyone and anything else. Seek Him first and keep the Lord Jesus first place in your life. Everything and everyone else comes secondary to the Lord. Where Jesus is, there is total victory; there are no losses in Christ. Jesus Christ always comes out victorious! Hallelujah!

# CHAPTER TWELVE

# Faith to Stand

Ephesians 6:10, 13, 14 says, "Finally, my brethren, be strong in the Lord and in the power of His might, Put on the whole armor of God, that you may be able to stand against the wiles of the devil." Verses 13–14: "Therefore take up the whole armor of God, that you may be able to withstand in the evil day, and having done all, to stand. Stand therefore, having girded your waist with truth, having put on the breastplate of righteousness, and having shod your feet with the preparation of the gospel of peace; above all, taking the shield of faith with which you will be able to quench all the fiery darts of the wicked one."

Faith to stand is faith that will not quit. It is faith that will not give in. It is faith that will not be moved. Even when times come when you want to give up or give in, there is something down on the inside of you that refuses to quit. There is something in you pushing you to persevere. There is something in you strengthening you to keep going, no matter how difficult it may seem; you persist in the good fight of faith. That something in you is the Spirit of the

Lord.

We cannot fight the good fight of faith without Jesus. Jesus Christ is our help in the fight. It's easy to give up. It's easy to quit. Sometimes quitting is a relief because perseverance often comes with pain. When you quit, the deception is that the pain will end because you no longer have to endure the task that may seem hard. But not living up to your God-given potential is where the real pain is; not living the life that Jesus purposed for you to live is more painful than any obstacle; it is greater than any challenge you may face. Not pursuing what God called you to do to bring Him glory is the greatest pain there is.

There is pain in moving forward, and there is pain in staying stuck. Moving forward can be painful, change can be difficult, but what is more painful is missing your God-given destiny; what is more painful is living a life less than God's best for you; what is more painful is living a life filled with regret. When the Lord calls you to pursue a dream He placed in you, and you put it off and put it off and put it off, ask yourself: "Why am I choosing not to move forward?"

The reason why people choose not to move forward is fear of failure. But guess what? It is better to try and fail than to not try at all; not trying at all is a failure just the same. It's easy to talk yourself out of something, to list all the reasons why it won't work out, but when God gives you the dream, He also gives you the strategy to fulfill the dream and turn your dream into reality. It will not be easy, it will not be without setbacks, but nothing worth having is ever easy. It will take hard work, it will take dedication, and it will take commitment on your part. You have to be determined to go after your dreams. You have to be committed and stay committed to going after the dream God gave you, even when you fail, even when you are told no, even when it does not work out the way you planned, you have to stay committed to following through. No matter how painful it may be, stay in faith and stand on the promises of God. Be persistent until you accomplish what you set out to do.

The enemy will whisper lies that you will not succeed in what God has called you to do; he will remind you of the times when you failed, the times when you quit, the times when it did not work, but pay him no mind. That is just a distraction to keep you hindered and in a place of lack. Instead, focus your thoughts on what the Lord says in His Word and continue to pursue your goals and aspirations. Galatians 6:9 in the Message Bible reads, "So let's not allow ourselves to get fatigued doing good. At the right time we will harvest a good crop if we don't give up, or quit." Whenever you are tempted to give up, whenever you are tempted to quit on yourself, be reminded of this verse. Notice in the text: "...*let's not allow ourselves to get fatigued*..." The statement to not allow ourselves to get fatigued indicates that we have a say, so we have a choice whether or not we quit. Sure, circumstances may come to hinder you, things may not always go the way you had in mind, but if you will stay the course and keep at it, your efforts will pay off—eventually. Be encouraged; the Lord rewards diligence.

To stand is to remain stable, to take up or maintain a specified position or course. To stand is to remain without being disturbed, to engage in, or to encounter. Faith to stand requires participation. You can have great faith, but if you are not working toward what you are believing God for, your faith is dead—no longer in use, valid, effective, or relevant. Faith to stand requires endurance, no matter what. No matter how long it takes, you choose to continue on, even in the face of adversity.

# CHAPTER THIRTEEN

# Obedience

Obedience is submission to God. It is an intentional choice to yield yourself to the Father. Obedience to the Father tells Him, "Lord, I'll do what You tell me to do, no matter what." Obedience to the Father essentially is love. John 14:15 reminds us, if we love God, to obey His commandments. It is easy to obey God when everything is going well in our lives. The real challenge is to obey God when enduring trials, to obey God when we do not "feel" like it, to obey God when there is uncertainty.

Obedience to God is not always easy; it takes discipline. There were many times in my life when I was disobedient to God. I was disobedient because I wanted to do what I wanted to do. I was disobedient to God because I was selfish. I wanted to have my way, even if the consequences meant separation from Him. Instead of yielding to Him, I yielded to my flesh. I allowed my emotions to lead me and disregarded being led by the Spirit of God. You cannot be in a real relationship with Christ when you are not obedient to Him. Disobedience to God is sin, and sin always separates one from Christ.

Romans 6:16–18 warns us, "Do you not know that to whom you present yourselves slaves to obey, you are that one's slaves whom you obey, whether of sin leading to death or of obedience leading to righteousness? But God be thanked that though you were slaves of sin, yet you obeyed from the heart that form of doctrine to which you were delivered. And having been set free from sin, you became slaves of righteousness."

Are you living in disobedience to the Lord? Is there something that God has warned you to turn away from? Has the Lord warned you to turn away from wrong habits or wrong thinking or wrong attitudes? Have you gone your own way despite the nudging of the Holy Spirit to follow His leading? Know this, as long as you choose to continue to live in disobedience to God, you will continue to live frustrated and in a state of inner turmoil.

There is no peace living in obstinacy to the will of God. Living outside of God's will creates instability. Living outside of God's will creates constant uncertainty because you have no assurance of the Lord's presence in your everyday life. Remember, sin separates you from Christ. But living in obedience to Christ gives the blessed assurance that you are in the center of His will, even when circumstances do not always go your way. It is better to allow the Lord to have His way and live in total security than to have your way unsure of where you stand with Him.

One way to stay in obedience to God is to stay in the Word of God. As mentioned in Chapter One, spending time in God's Word on a daily basis will give you instructions on what to do and what not to do in any given situation. Staying in the Word of God will keep you in constant communion with the Father. Staying in the Word of God will keep Jesus at the forefront of your everyday life and lead you into a more intimate relationship with Him. When you are truly in relationship with the Lord, you want to be obedient to Him and yield yourself to Him completely. When you are truly in relationship with Him, your desires become what He desires for you.

There is no issue outside of the knowledge of Jesus Christ. The Holy Spirit will speak directly to your situation and provide a way of escape for you when you trust Him. Trusting God is not an easy task. It takes courage to trust God. But if you want to live a life of obedience to the Lord, you have to trust Him. There is no other way. You cannot live in obedience to Jesus if you do not trust Him at all times. When you trust the Lord, you have the desire to keep Him first because it is more important to you to allow Him to have His way rather than your own. It is more important to you that Jesus be magnified than self. Obedience is not selfish; it is self*less*. John 3:30 explains, "He must increase, but I *must decrease*." The Message Bible Version explains it like this: "This is the assigned moment for him to move into the center, while I slip off to the sidelines."

Obedience to God exalts Christ and lowers our own

estimation. Disobedience exalts self. Disobedience is self-serving; it serves one's own interests. Disobedience has no concern for the needs of others. Being self-serving is preoccupied with one's own interests and often disregards the truth. Being self-centered is all about "me." It makes no room for God. We are not higher than God. His ways are higher than our ways, and His thoughts are higher than our thoughts (Isaiah 55:9). A life of obedience to Christ is a blessed life.

# CHAPTER FOURTEEN

# Gratitude, Grace, and God's Favor

Gratitude is the state of being grateful. Gratitude is thankfulness. A heart of gratitude is appreciative. Are you grateful to the Lord Jesus? The more you open your heart to gratitude unto the Father, the more you will recognize the presence of the Lord Jesus in everything. One of the names of God is Jehovah-Shammah; the Lord is *there*; the Lord is *present* (see Ezekiel 48:35). Recognizing that the Lord is always *there*, that He is ever *present* makes your heart glad because you trust that He is always with you; because you recognize that you are constantly in His presence. In His presence, there is fullness of joy (Psalm 16:11).

Do you thank God for His goodness in your life? Do you thank Him for the favor He blesses you with? God's favor toward His people is grace. Grace is God's unmerited favor. It is unmerited because we do not deserve His grace. It is unmerited because we cannot earn it, but it is freely given to us by Him because of how good He is, not how good we are. We can never be "good enough" to earn the grace of God.

Oftentimes, there is the distorted belief that we need to earn God's love or that we need to earn His approval in order for Him to accept us. But that could not be further from the truth. God's love for us is not contingent on our behavior or our works. "But if it is by grace, it is no longer on the basis of works; otherwise grace would no longer be grace" (Romans 11:6). His love toward us is based on who He is because He is *LOVE* (1 John 4:16). And because God is love, He is full of grace toward us as well. The grace of God is His compassion and kindness toward us because He is filled with love for us that never runs out or wax cold [His love is not waning].

An attitude of gratitude to the Lord will help you to recognize how loving our heavenly Father is. When we have a heart of gratitude toward Jesus, we thank Him for how good He is, we thank Him for loving us in spite of us, we thank Him for accepting us, even when we were separated from Him by our sins. The desire to show gratitude to the Lord cannot be helped because it is our spirit that desires to love Him, and by loving Him, we show appreciation to Him. When you love someone, you appreciate who they are to you.

*"For by grace you have been saved through
faith, and that not of yourselves; it is the gift
of God, not of works, lest anyone should*

*boast. For we are His workmanship, created in Christ Jesus for good works, which God prepared beforehand that we should walk in them. "*

**Ephesians 2:8–10**

Ever since I was a little girl, my mother taught me the importance of gratitude. She instilled in me to always show gratitude to others, especially when I received a gift or something "special." As an only child, I got practically everything I ever wanted from my parents. Sure, my mother told me no sometimes, but for the most part, my mother provided me with anything and everything I asked for if she had the means to do so. And it was very seldom that I asked for anything; because my mother would give to me so freely and without hesitation I did not feel the need to. She gave of her time, emotionally and financially, to me in every way. The great part about how my mother treated me was that she did not overdo it. She did not overcompensate in her love for me by giving of material possessions. My mother gave to me from her heart and not out of obligation. She is a cheerful giver—God loves a cheerful giver (2 Corinthians 9:6–7).

The Lord also freely gives to us as His children. He blesses us with divine favor. Divine favor that is freely given to us by God grants us the redemption of sin. When Jesus Christ laid down His life for us, He settled it all. His death on the cross redeemed us from sin and death. His death on the cross atoned for our sins. He bore our sins in

His own body. He saved us from death, hell, and the grave. It is by grace that we are saved, not anything of ourselves, but it is God's unmerited favor toward us that all be saved. It is not the Lord's will that any should perish, but all to come to repentance (2 Peter 3:8–10). It is God's will for us to have everlasting life, which can only come by accepting Christ in our hearts, by acknowledging that Jesus Christ is LORD, and by acknowledging His death and resurrection. Christ's death on the cross is a gift to all of us. Whether received or not, it is a gift. Salvation is a gift from the Lord. The gift of salvation is the ultimate expression of love bestowed upon us from the Father through Christ.

Second Corinthians 6:1–2 in the Amplified Bible says, "Working together with Him, we strongly urge you not to receive God's grace in vain [by turning away sound doctrine and His merciful kindness]. For He says, AT THE ACCEPTABLE TIME (the time of grace) I LISTENED TO YOU, AND I HELPED YOU ON THE DAY OF SALVATION." Behold, now is "THE ACCEPTABLE TIME. Behold, now is "THE DAY OF SALVATION."

If you have never trusted Jesus Christ as your personal Savior, say this prayer with me:

## Prayer of Salvation

*"Lord Jesus, I am a sinner. I confess my sins known and unknown. I repent of my sins. I believe that You died on the cross for me, went*

*to hell and the grave, and was raised again on the third day by the glory of the Father, and You are now seated at the right hand of the Father in heavenly places. I accept You as my Lord and my Savior. Shape me and mold me according to Your Word, to be who You called me to be. Amen."*

The grace of God is His loving kindness toward us. Think back over your life and recall the times when you made foolish decisions that could have resulted in disaster, but the grace of God kept you. Think back over your life and recall the times when you made the choice to go your own way instead of going in the direction the Lord was calling you to, but His grace redirected you and changed your position from where you were headed. Your life could have gone another way if it had not been for God's grace that covered you had it not been for His unmerited favor on your life. Walk it out with Jesus and allow His grace to be the guiding force to get you to the place the Lord destined you to be. The grace of God has kept you this far, and His grace will lead you home.

> *"...For there is no difference; for all have sinned and fall short of the glory of God, being justified freely by His grace through the redemption that is in Christ Jesus, whom God set forth as a propitiation by His blood, through faith, to demonstrate His righteousness, because in His forbearance God had passed over the sins that were*

*previously committed, to demonstrate at the present time His righteousness, that He might be just and the justifier of the one who has faith in Jesus."*

**Romans 3:22–26**

# CHAPTER FIFTEEN

# Walking in Love

The Scripture instructs us in 1 Corinthians 13:1–13;

*"Though I speak with the tongues of men and of angels, but have not love, I have become sounding brass or a clanging cymbal. And though I have the gift of prophecy, and understand all mysteries and all knowledge, and though I have all faith, so that I could remove mountains, but have not love, I am nothing. And though I bestow all my goods to feed the poor, and though I give my body to be burned, but have not love, it profits me nothing. Love suffers long and is kind; love does not envy; love does not parade itself, is not puffed up; does not behave rudely, does not seek its own, is not provoked, thinks no evil; does not rejoice in iniquity, but rejoices in the truth; bears all things, believes all things, hopes all things, endures all things. Love never fails. But whether there are prophecies, they will fail; whether there are tongues, they will cease;*

*whether there is knowledge, it will vanish away. For we know in part and we prophesy in part. But when that which is perfect has come, then that which is in part will be done away. When I was a child, I spoke as a child, I understood as a child, I thought as a child; but when I became a man, I put away childish things. For now we see in a mirror, dimly, but then face to face. Now I know in part, but then I shall know just as I also am known. And now abide faith, hope, love, these three; but the greatest of these is love."*

I admittedly do not always walk in love toward my fellow man and even toward those in my household, toward my own children. Verse 4 talks about how love suffers long. In the King James Version, to suffer long is patience. The text says, "Love is not rude." Those are two issues that I have a weakness in; being patient and not being rude. I am not always patient toward other people, and when I choose to be impatient, in turn, I can be rather rude and oftentimes dismissive. I have found that the times when I am rude and impatient is when I am angry or when I am tired. [It is important to recognize what triggers those behaviors. When you recognize your areas of weakness, then you can turn those weaknesses over to the Lord in prayer and allow Him to deal with those weaknesses and deal with you]. I behave rudely and impatiently during those times because instead of choosing to remain in love no matter how I feel, I inadvertently allow my emotions to affect my behavior.

Love is not always about a "feeling," but walking in love is about how we treat others. Love is about action. It is a conscious decision to willingly act out a deed, no matter how we may feel. Love is kind means having or showing a friendly, generous, sympathetic, or warm-hearted nature. To be kind is to be considerate and courteous. Kindness is one of the fruits of the Spirit (see Galatians 5:22).

When we allow our emotions to dictate our behavior, it is easy to get out of love because we are allowing our flesh to have its way. And that does not mean that you are a bad person or a bad parent; it does not mean that you do not care about your children or other people, but what that exposes is a weakness in you that only God can correct. Weaknesses in your character can be changed when you design your heart to be changed. "Create in me a clean heart, O God; and renew a right spirit within me" (Psalm 51:10). How can the Lord create a clean heart in you, you ask? You will see your heart begin to change when you turn those issues of weakness over to the Lord in prayer, when you allow His Word to transform your heart and transform your mind. It is not a one-time event but a continuous journey with God.

When you get out of love, acknowledge it right away. It is not something that you are oblivious to. We all know when we are rude or impatient. Even before the Holy Spirit points it out to you, in your heart, you are already aware of it. When you behave in a way not pleasing to God, confess it, repent of it, and search out what the Word says about it. Study the Word in the areas of your life where you have weakness. The Word will not only convict you, but the Word will change you on the inside when you yield yourself to God—God's Word is transformative.

When God convicts us of our behavior, He points out to us or makes us aware of a wrong action or of a wrong-doing. Correction from the Lord is always a good thing. Conviction of the Holy Spirit always leads to something better for you, be it a better attitude or a better mindset or better choices. The Holy Spirit will always lead you to better, but it is up to you to do better. You cannot do better in your own strength or in your own might; you must allow the Spirit of God to work in you as only He can. It takes surrendering to Jesus daily.

Surrendering to God is to relinquish control to Him. If you exhibit controlling behavior, it is difficult to walk in love. There is a major difference in being in control and being controlling. I have found myself being controlling toward others to appease my own anxiety in a situation. If a situation made me anxious or fearful, I had an overwhelming need to control my environment. A controlling person is a fearful person. Nobody wants to live with or be around a person who is controlling. It is a displeasing attribute in one's life. Relinquishing control to the Lord Jesus frees us from the burden of worry because we trust that God is in total control. He has total dominion. "... far above all rule and authority and power and dominion [whether angelic or human], and [far above] every name that is named [above every title that can be conferred], not only in this age *and* world but also in the one to come. And He put all things [in every realm] in subjection under Christ's feet, and appointed Him as [supreme and authoritative] head over all things in the church, which is His body, the fullness of Him who fills *and* completes all things in all [believers]." (Ephesians 1:21–23 AMP)

We trust that He is sovereign, which means He has supreme authority over everyone and everything, and nothing is out of His reach. When we keep our mind stayed on Jesus and not on our worries or our fears, He will keep us in perfect peace (Isaiah 25:3). When you are constantly trying to control everything around you, there is no real peace on the inside. Real peace only comes from being in relationship with the Lord and trusting Him with your whole heart. As previously mentioned, walking in love requires trusting God.

# CHAPTER SIXTEEN

## Surrender

Surrendering to the Lord is easier said than done. As mentioned in Chapter Fifteen, surrendering to God is to relinquish control to Jesus on a daily basis. Surrendering to the Lord is to allow yourself to be yielded to His divine will. Surrendering to the Lord is to lay down your will for the will of God. When we surrender to Christ, we are submitting to His power and His authority; we give up what we may think or desire for what Christ thinks and what He desires for us. The opposite of surrender is resistance. It is never wise to be in resistance to God. When we choose resistance, we are in opposition to God. The only one who we should resist is the devil. The enemy is in opposition to Christ. The enemy is against God. If we choose to live in resistance or in opposition to God, we are behaving like the devil. Every child of God must surrender and submit to the Lord. You cannot surrender a little bit; you have to be all in with Jesus. Surrendering to Jesus is the only way to live a victorious life in Christ. Any other decision is foolish and will ultimately result in destruction.

First Peter 5:6–11 in the Amplified Bible says:

*"Therefore humble yourselves under the mighty hand of God [set aside self-righteous pride], so that He may exalt you [to a place of honor in His service] at the appropriate time, casting all your cares [all your anxieties, all your worries, and all your concerns, once and for all] on Him, for He cares about you [with deepest affection, and watches over you very carefully]. Be sober [well balanced and self-disciplined], be alert and cautious at all times. That enemy of yours, the devil, prowls around like a roaring lion [fiercely hungry], seeking someone to devour. But resist him, be firm in your faith [against his attack – rooted, established, immovable], knowing that the same experiences of suffering are being experienced by your brothers and sisters throughout the world. [You do not suffer alone.] After you have suffered for a little while, the God of all grace [who imparts His blessing and favor], who called you to His own eternal glory in Christ, will Himself complete, confirm, strengthen, and establish you [making you what you ought to be]. To Him be dominion (power, authority, sovereignty) forever and ever. Amen."*

Look at all of the benefits that come from surrendering to Christ. Surrendering to Christ honors Him. Surrendering to Christ prepares us to serve Him with humility.

Surrendering to Christ allows us to be free of holding onto anxieties and worries and all of our cares. Surrendering to Christ enables us to set aside self-pride and acknowledge His sovereignty in our lives (we do not know better than the Lord). Surrendering to Christ allows Jesus to watch over us. Surrendering to Christ grants provision (God provides for us; He takes care of us). Surrendering to Christ grants protection (being in the will of God protects us from the plans of the enemy). Surrendering to Christ blesses us with favor (the favor of God is an impartation bestowed to us from the Lord; He grants us wisdom). Surrendering to Christ strengthens us to resist the enemy (we are strengthened by Jesus to stand firm in our faith in Him and in our faith in His Word, that no matter how the enemy attacks us, because we are surrendered to Jesus, the devil cannot have his way in our lives). Surrendering to Christ assures us that we are never alone (God is always with us. In every circumstance of life, He is with us). Surrendering to Christ reassures us that God will make us who we ought to be, that we will become who He created us to be, and it is all for His glory.

# Reflection Is Introspective

Ask yourself the following questions:

Do I have difficulty surrendering to Jesus?

Why am I resistant to fully surrendering to the Lord?

What is it in my life that I am hesitant to surrender to the Lord?

Is my way better than the Lord's way?

What am I afraid of?

Am I afraid of God?

How do I view God?

Do I believe that Jesus can take care of me in every situation?

Do I trust Jesus?

Do I believe the Word of God in its entirety?

Do I have faith that God's Word is for me?

Do I believe I am forgiven?

Do I live in regret of past decisions?

What anxieties and worries do I have?

How can I learn to trust Jesus more?

Do I believe that God loves me?

Consider the above questions. Be honest in your responses. First, ask the Lord to direct your heart in His Word regarding the questions asked. What does the Word say regarding these issues? Search your Bible Index. Second, write out your answers and then ponder on your responses to the questions asked. Third, ask the Lord to give you revelation on your responses. What did the Word of God reveal to you regarding your responses? After that, ask Him to fill your mind with the truth of Who He is, what His Word declares, and how to apply His Word in the areas of your life where you have doubt. Subsequently, ask the Lord to strengthen your heart to trust Him more and more. Lastly, thank the Lord for His wisdom and for His omniscience. God is all-knowing. There is not one subject that He does not have infinite knowledge of. There is not one issue of life that He cannot guide you in. Nothing is beyond His wisdom. God knows it all.

Some have a false belief that we should not question God, but that is simply not scriptural. The Bible tells us in James 1:5–6, "If any of you lacks wisdom, let him ask of God, who gives to all liberally and without reproach, and it will be given to him." Understanding God's will requires seeking Him out, and when we seek Him, we ask questions, we pray for revelation and knowledge of His Word, and we trust Him for godly wisdom. That does not mean that God will always answer us as soon as we ask Him, but by faith and by staying in His Word, eventually, the Holy Spirit will reveal mysteries to us, according to His will and not our want. Surrendering to God requires steadfast and immovable faith in Him.

Having faith in God is a process. Wouldn't it be wonderful if we never had any doubts? Wouldn't it be awesome if we always walked by faith and never wavered? What's wonderful about how loving our heavenly Father is, is that He knows that we will struggle with times of uncertainty and with times of doubt. He knows how many times we may faint in our mind and grow weary. He is aware of all our shortcomings, and yet He loves us anyway. He gives us more chances than we deserve. The Lord does not forsake us in our weaknesses. The Lord is so gracious toward us. He is ever faithful. Even when we turn our back on Him, He still loves us and still desires to be in relationship with us. He loves us with *true* unconditional love, not as the world *loves*. His unconditional love toward us will not allow us to stay the way we came to Him, but by His grace, He transforms us day by day by day. Love seeks the best for others (1 John 4:7, AMP). God is long-suffering toward us—He is incredibly patient toward us. How can we not surrender to such a loving and caring Father? His patience toward us is the epitome of kindness and love. He is the good, good Father. He is perfect in every way.

# CHAPTER SEVENTEEN

# The Lord, My Shield and My Buckler

*"The LORD is my light and my salvation—
Whom shall I fear? The LORD is the refuge
and fortress of my life—Whom shall I dread?
When the wicked came against me to eat up
my flesh, My adversaries and my enemies,
they stumbled and fell. Though an army
encamp against me, My heart will not fear;
Though war arise against me, Even in this I
am confident. One thing I have asked of the
LORD and that I will seek: That I may dwell
in the house of the LORD [in His presence]
all the days of my life, To gaze upon the
beauty [the delightful loveliness and majestic
grandeur] of the LORD And to meditate in
His temple. For in the day of trouble He will
hide me in His shelter; In the secret place of
His tent He will hide me; He will lift me up
on a rock. And now my head will be lifted up
above my enemies around me, In His tent I will*

*offer sacrifices with shouts of joy; I will sing, yes, I will sing praises to the LORD. Hear, O LORD, when I cry aloud; Be gracious and compassionate to me and answer me. When You said, "Seek My face [in prayer, require My presence as your greatest need], "my heart said to You, "Your face, O LORD, I will seek [on the authority of Your word]. Do not hide Your face from me, Do not turn Your servant away in anger; You have been my help; Do not abandon me nor, leave me, O God of my salvation! Although my father and my mother have abandoned me, Yet the LORD will take me up [adopt me as His child]. Teach me Your way, O LORD, And lead me on a level path Because of my enemies [who lie in wait]. Do not give me up to the will of my adversaries, For false witnesses have come against me; They breathe out violence. I would have despaired had I not believed that I would see the goodness of the LORD In the land of the living. Wait for and confidently expect the LORD; Be strong and let your heart take courage; Yes, wait for and confidently expect the LORD."*

**Psalm 27 (AMP)**

Psalm 27 is about having fearless trust in God, written by King David. The Psalms is a book of prayers, praises, instrumental music, songs, and poetry to the Lord. The Psalmist David thanked God for deliverance from personal distresses. King David was the third king of the United

Monarchy of Israel and Judah. David started out as a young shepherd boy and harpist who gained notability (fame) for slaying the giant Goliath with a slingshot and five smooth stones. Goliath was a champion of the Philistines in southern Canaan, an enemy of the Israelite people.

We all have an enemy, and his name is Satan. Satan is an enemy to God's people (to all people). Satan is the god of this world. He is the wicked one and evil in all his ways. Satan is the force behind all evil committed by mankind in this world; he is the source behind all things demonic. The devil is the great (extreme) deceiver (Revelation 12:9). Instead of coming against people who do wrong, we need to come against the devil because it is the devil that uses people to do his dirty work. The devil has no new tricks. The same tactics that he used in biblical days are the same tactics that he uses now. The same deceptions that he used against Eve in the Garden, he uses today.

The devil's plan of action is to halt the purposes and plans of God. The enemy comes against us with lies so that we will not trust in God. The enemy desires to steal our faith in God so that he can ultimately steal our life and prevail against us. Jesus Christ is greater than the devil. Jesus Christ has all dominion and all power in His hands. The enemy can only do what God allows him to do, and remember, as previously mentioned, the Lord allows the enemy to come against us when we choose to sin, when we choose to walk in fear instead of faith, and when we choose to allow ourselves to be separated from God through disobedience. Disobedience blocks the flow of God in our lives. But even when the Lord allows the enemy to oppose us, He allows the adversity so that we come back into alignment with Him and grow in relationship to Jesus.

Jesus Christ reigns, and He rules. The devil is powerless against the Lord. The devil is powerless against the Name of Jesus. Demons tremble and bow at the Name of Jesus. The Lord's Name is a shield against all evil. The enemy is powerless against those who are in Christ and those who depend on the Lord Jesus to be their Shield and their Buckler. The enemy is powerless against those who walk uprightly in obedience to God. The weapons of the enemy may be formed, but walking in obedience before the Lord provides protection; so, even though the weapons may be formed, they will not prosper.

A shield provides protection; it protects against hurt, harm, and danger; it protects against attacks; it covers; it conceals; it intercepts; a shield defends. A shield is a broad piece of armor. A shield blocks. A shield is a shelter. The Lord is our Shelter; He hides us in the secret place; He is our Refuge and our Fortress; He covers us with His feathers, and under His wings, we can take refuge (Psalm 91).

When I think back over my life and remember all of the times I endured great opposition and faced all sorts of hurt, harm, and danger, but the Lord did not allow the gates of hell to prevail against me, the Lord did not allow me to be swallowed up and destroyed, I cannot help but give

God glory. My soul wants to praise Him. My soul wants to worship Him. My soul wants to thank Him, and my soul wants to cry out, "Hallelujah!" Hallelujah to Jesus for His love and His goodness! Hallelujah to Jesus for His mercy and His grace! Hallelujah to Jesus for His forgiveness of my sins! Hallelujah to Jesus for deliverance and healing! Hallelujah to Jesus for His covering! Hallelujah to Jesus for His hand on my life! Hallelujah to Jesus for His presence in my life, even when I turned my back on Him!

The Lord kept me even when I was living for me, myself, and I. He kept me for Himself so that one day He could use me for His purpose and His plan in the earth. He kept me so that one day I would consider my sinful ways and repent and pray and confess that Jesus Christ is Lord of my life. I am nothing without the Lord Jesus Christ in my life. Apart from Him, I can do nothing, but through Him, I can do all things because He strengthens me. Christ is my Shield and my Buckler! He shields me from the evil one. The truth of His Word is my Buckler. The Word of God is my armor against the lies of the enemy. The Word of God intercedes for me. When the enemy accuses me day and night before Him, God says, "Not guilty." When the enemy asks to have me and sift me like wheat, God says, "Touch not My anointed and do My prophet no harm." When the enemy calls me guilty, God says, "I have been redeemed by the shedding of the Blood of Jesus." When the enemy comes in like a flood and tries to swallow me up and destroy me, the truth of God's Word grips my soul and reminds me who I am in Christ. I am a daughter of the Most High God. I am a daughter of the King of kings and the Lord of lords. I am accepted in the Beloved. I am His masterpiece, created in His image and in His likeness. I am created to worship and adore the Lord Jesus. I am victorious through Christ. I am not a victim. I am an overcomer through Christ. I am the head and not the tail. I am above only and not beneath. I am His! And so are you!

When we put our faith in God, when we open our hearts to Him, when we surrender our lives to Jesus and recognize that He truly is our Shield and our Buckler, we can live with such security and such hope because we know *Who* we belong to.

When we know who we belong to and begin to understand the faithfulness of God, our perception begins to change. We will walk differently—with confidence. We will speak differently—speaking words of faith and not words of defeat. We will react differently—resting in the peace of God, trusting and believing that all circumstances we endure are working for our good. We will love differently—treating others with kindness and patience. Loving others even when we feel it is undeserved. We will love our enemies, bless those who curse us, do good to those who hate us, and pray for those who spitefully use us and persecute us. We will love like God loves. We will begin to imitate our heavenly Father and walk in His ways because the Holy Spirit enables us to do so. We will begin to yield ourselves to the Father and His will, and we will begin to renounce our desires for what God desires for us. We will be changed because the love of God flows through us because we are anchored in Christ—our Shield and our Buckler—the One Who holds us together when we would most assuredly fall apart without Him.

# CHAPTER EIGHTEEN

# Purpose and Destiny

We all have a purpose and a destiny to fulfill in this life. There is something special that each of us was created to accomplish for the glory of God. The sad thing is that not everyone fulfills their God-given purpose, either because they refuse to walk in the purposes and plan of God or because they allow fear to rob them of their destiny or because they reject Jesus Christ as Lord of their life. There is no God-given purpose apart from being in relationship with Christ. Talent does not equal anointing. Anointing is of God. Without the anointing of God, we cannot fulfill what He created us to do. A person can have great talents and abilities, but if those talents and abilities are not utilized for the glory of God, they are of no effect for the kingdom of God.

To be anointed is to be divinely chosen; it is to be chosen officially; it is to receive a special calling from God for His plan and His purpose; to be anointed is to be consecrated (set apart) and empowered by the Holy Spirit to do the work of the Lord here on earth. Every born-again believer has a God-given purpose, and as soon as we trusted Jesus as our Savior, that purpose was brought out of hibernation.

As disciples of Christ, we are to be the hands and feet of Jesus here in the earth. Remember what Ephesians 2:10 encourages *that we are God's workmanship, created in Christ Jesus for good works, which God prepared beforehand that we should walk in them.* We are to carry on the ministry that Jesus began. We are to allow Christ to live His life through us. We are vessels for the Gospel of Jesus Christ to be commissioned to those around us—known and unknown. We are all influencing somebody with how we live our lives. There is something that all of us are exceptional at, and it is not of our own volition. But it is divinely predetermined by God before the foundation of the world. Before God formed us in our mother's womb, He knew us, and before we were born, He set us apart... (see Jeremiah 1:5).

Think of some things that you are very good at or something that you have a deep passion for. That is your purpose and destiny from God. We are not all called to be pastors or prophets or apostles, but we are all called to minister to others however God desires. We are all here to help or care or attend to the needs of someone else. We are all called to serve as agents of change in the Body of Christ. We are all called to carry out a specific function in the Body of Christ. The Body of Christ refers to those who heard the Word of Truth, the Gospel of our salvation, believed in Jesus as Lord and Savior and were sealed with the promise of the Holy Spirit. Be it in business or in your home with your children, we are all called to glorify God with the talents, gifts, and abilities He blessed us with.

Anointing gives God the glory, not us. Anointing showcases the God in us, not our own "greatness." Anointing lifts up the Name of Jesus, not our own. Anointing gives Christ the standing ovation, not us. Jesus Christ is our example; we are to model our lives after Him. The reason we are all here is to worship, praise, and glorify the Lord Jesus. It is not about us and how we can be seen. It is about Christ and how He can be magnified here in the earth. We are all here to be in relationship with the Father through the Son. That is why Christ died for us so that through Him we might be saved. I say *might* because we have free will. The Lord provided us the free gift of salvation, but it is our choice to accept Jesus as our personal Savior. A gift cannot be received unless it is first accepted. *Selah*—pause and think on that.

Ephesians 1 in the Amplified says:

> *"Paul, an apostle (special messenger, personally chosen representative) of Christ Jesus (the Messiah, the Anointed), by the will of God [that is, by His purpose and choice], To the saints (God's people) who are at Ephesus and are faithful and loyal and steadfast in Christ Jesus: Grace to you and peace [inner calm and spiritual well-being] from God our Father and the Lord Jesus Christ. Blessed*

*and worthy of praise be the God and Father of our Lord Jesus Christ, who has blessed us with every spiritual blessing in the heavenly realms in Christ [actually selected us for Himself as His own] before the foundation of the world, so that we would be holy [that is, consecrated, set apart for Him, purpose-driven] and blameless in His sight. In love He predestined and lovingly planned for us to be adopted to Himself as [His own] children through Jesus Christ, in accordance with the kind intention and good pleasure of His will—to the praise of His glorious grace and favor, which He so freely bestowed on us in the Beloved [His Son, Jesus Christ]. In Him we have redemption [that is, our deliverance and salvation] through His blood, [which paid the penalty for our sin and resulted in] the forgiveness and complete pardon of our sin, in accordance with the riches of His grace which He lavished on us. In all wisdom and understanding [with practical insight] He made known to us the mystery of His will according to His good pleasure, which He purposed in Christ, with regard to the fulfillment of the times [that is the end of history, the climax of the ages]—to bring all things together in Christ, [both] things in the heavens and things on the earth. In Him, you also, when you heard the word of truth, the good news of your salvation, and [as a result] believed in Him, were stamped with the seal of the promised Holy Spirit [the One promised by Christ] as owned and protected [by God]. The Spirit is the guarantee [the first installment, the pledge, a foretaste] of our inheritance until the redemption of God's own [purchased] possession [His believers], to the praise of His glory. For this reason, because I have heard of your faith in the Lord Jesus and your love for all God's people, I do not cease to give thanks for you, remembering you in my prayers; [that the God of our Lord Jesus Christ, the Father of glory, may grant you a spirit of wisdom and of revelation [that gives you a deep and personal and intimate insight] into the true knowledge of Him [for we know the Father through the Son]. And [I pray] that the eyes of your heart [the very center and core of your being] may be enlightened [flooded with light by the Holy Spirit], so that you will know and cherish the hope [the divine guarantee, the confident expectation] to which He has called you, the riches of His glorious inheritance in the saints (God's people, and [so that you will begin to know] what the immeasurable and unlimited and surpassing greatness of His [active, spiritual] power is in us who believe. These are in accordance with the working of His mighty strength which He produced in Christ when He raised Him from the dead and seated Him at His own right hand in the heavenly places, far above all rule and authority and power and dominion [whether angelic or human], and [far above] every name that is named [above every title that can be conferred], not only in this age and world but also in the one to come. And He put all things [in every realm] in subjection under Christ's feet, and appointed Him as [supreme and authoritative] head over all things in the church, which is His body, the fullness of Him who fills and completes all things in all [believers]."*

Have you discovered God's purpose for your life? What is it that you are good at? What is it that you do exceptionally well? What is it that you are passionate about? As a born-again believer, those talents, gifts, and abilities are to be used for the glory of our Lord Jesus Christ. We are all gifted in some kind of way. Perhaps you have a passion for teaching children, or maybe you have always desired to teach and help to shape our youth. That is your God-given gift. Or maybe you have a merciful way about you, and you have the gift of healing or caring for the sick; working in medicine as a nurse or a doctor or a therapist is your God-given gift. Or it could be that you play an instrument exceptionally well, you have been playing since childhood, your heart is filled with such joy when you hear a melody or feel the vibrations of an instrument being played; then, music may be your God-given gift.

Gifts are to be shared with others, not kept for ourselves. When you give your gift back to the world, you are actually giving those gifts back to the Lord, Who designed you for His purpose. Do not sit on the gifts that God has blessed you with; utilize those gifts, live them out with the leading of the Holy Spirit, and your gifts will make room for you and bring you before great men (Proverbs 18:16).

You have probably heard the saying, "Life is short," but actually, life is not short. The issue is that, oftentimes, we wait too long to live the life we ought to live, a life of purpose and intentionality. Consider how terribly sad and regretful it must be to come to the end of life and realize you have not become who you were created to be. Think of how heart-wrenching it may be for God to reveal to you on that day what you could have been, what you could have done, who you could have helped, how you could have impacted the world around you. Well, the good news is that if you still have breath in your body, you still have purpose in God. The question is: What are you going to do with the time you have left? There is potential in you that you have not even tapped into yet. There are dreams that the Lord has placed in your heart that have lain dormant for years. Now is the time to wake those dreams and aspirations up again. Now is the time to run your race. Now is the time to write the vision and make it plain. "...For the vision is yet for an appointed [future] time. It hurries toward the goal [of fulfillment]; it will not fail. Even though it delays, wait [patiently] for it, Because it will certainly come; it will not delay" (Habakkuk 2:2–3, AMP).

# CHAPTER NINETEEN

# Humility

One of the fruits of the Spirit is meekness, which is humility. Jesus humbled Himself and went to the cross to die for you and for me. He humbled Himself and became obedient to *the point* of death, even the death of the cross (see Philippians 2:5–8). Humility is to have a modest opinion of our own importance or rank. Humility is to have a lack of false pride. False pride is an exaggeratedly high or pretentious opinion of oneself. Proverbs 8:13 reminds us, "The fear of the LORD *is* to hate evil; Pride and arrogance and the evil way…" The Lord abhors (hates) pride and arrogance. "…God resists the proud, But gives grace to the humble" (James 4:6).

The Bible says humility cures worldliness. Worldliness concerns itself with affairs of the world and neglects spiritual matters or needs. But the Bible reminds us that, as believers, we are in the world but not of the world (John 17:14–16). When we walk humbly before the Lord, we are Spirit-led. But when we walk in pride, we are self-led. Pride is what got Satan cast out of heaven. *Selah*—pause and think on that.

In James 4:10, it reads, "Humble yourselves in the sight of the Lord, and He will lift you up." Proverbs 3:33–34 reads, "The curse of the LORD *is* on the house of the wicked, But He blesses the home of the just. Surely He scorns the scornful, But gives grace to the humble." First John 2:16 reads, "For all that *is* in the world—the lust of the flesh, the lust of the eyes, and the pride of life—is not of the Father but is of the world. And the world is passing away, and the lust of it; but he who does the will of God abides forever." Proverbs 11:2 in the Amplified reads, "When pride comes [boiling up with an arrogant attitude of self-importance], then come dishonor *and* shame, But with the humble [the teachable who have been chiseled by trial and who have learned to walk humbly with God] there is wisdom *and* soundness of mind."

It is impossible to walk with God without walking humbly before Him. To walk humbly is to admit we need God. To walk humbly is to renounce our way for God's way. To walk humbly is to be yielded to the Spirit of God in all our ways. We cannot be Spirit-led with a heart of pride. "Pride *goes* before destruction, And a haughty spirit before a fall. Better *to be* of a humble spirit with the lowly, Than to divide the spoil with the proud" (Proverbs 16:18–19).

There have been countless times in my life when I thought I knew best, and as a result, I went my own way instead of considering God's way; that is pride. I often made up my mind too quickly and refused to heed God's warning in situations because I wanted to do what I wanted to do; that is pride. Pride is sin. Pride is selfishness and self-centeredness. It cannot be all about you when living a life poured out for Jesus. Jesus Christ has to be first place in our lives. He has to be considered when making important decisions. He has to be at the center of our lives; everything else must revolve around Him. We must submit to the will of God and be obedient to Him no matter what we think, how we feel, or what we desire. Our will must align with His will for us. Our desires must align with what He desires for us. Whenever you are uncertain of what His will and desire is in a situation, seek Him in His Word, and the Lord will speak to your heart concerning the matter.

Humility is a virtue. It is the quality of doing what is right and avoiding what is wrong. We can do right even when we may feel wrong. When we knowingly do the wrong thing, that is rebellion against God. Rebelling against God is sin because it is deliberate disobedience. Acts of sin first begin in the mind. When you continually think on sinful thoughts and do not bring those thoughts into captivity to the obedience of Christ (see 2 Corinthians 10:54), eventually, you will act on those thoughts.

The Apostle Paul put it like this:

> *"For what I am doing, I do not understand.*
> *For what I will to do, that I do not practice;*
> *but what I hate, that I do. If then, I do what*

*I will not to do, I agree with the law that it is good. But now, it is no longer I who do it, but sin that dwells in me. For I know that in me (that is, in my flesh) nothing good dwells; for to will is present with me, but how to perform what is good I do not find. For the good that I will to do, I do not do; but the evil I will not to do, that I practice. Now if I do what I will not to do, it is no longer I who do it, but sin that dwells in me. I find then a law, that evil is present with me, the one who wills to do good. For I delight in the law of God according to the inward man. But I see another law in my members, warring against the law of my mind, and bringing me into captivity to the law of sin which is in my members. O wretched man that I am! Who will deliver me from this body of death? I thank God—through Jesus Christ our Lord! So then, with the mind I myself serve the law of God, but with the flesh the law of sin."*

**Romans 7:15–25**

Walking humbly before God is worship. It is reverence to the Lord. Humility tells God, "Lord, I choose to be obedient to You and humble myself under Your authority." Walking humbly before God is showing our love for Him— it is respect to the Father. You cannot truly love God if you do not humble yourself before Him and honor Him because of who He is: our Lord, our Savior, our Father, and our Friend.

# CHAPTER TWENTY

# *Anchored in Christ*

*"In the same way God, in His desire to show
to the heirs of the promise the unchangeable
nature of His purpose, intervened and
guaranteed it with an oath, so that by two
unchangeable things [His promise and His
oath] in which it is impossible for God to lie,
we who have fled [to Him] for refuge would
have strong encouragement and indwelling
strength to hold tightly to the hope set before
us. This hope [this confident assurance] we
have as an anchor of the soul [it cannot slip
and it cannot break down under whatever
pressure bears upon it]—a safe and steadfast
hope that enters within the veil [of the heavenly
temple, that most Holy Place in which the
very presence of God dwells], where Jesus
has entered [in advance] as a forerunner
for us, having become a High Priest forever
according to the order of Melchizedek."*

**Hebrews 6:17–20 (AMP)**

The Lord Jesus is our forerunner. He goes before us. The
Scripture reminds us in Deuteronomy 31:8 that the Lord is

the One Who goes before us, that He will not leave us nor forsake us, and we are not to be afraid or dismayed. The Amplified Bible says that He will be with us. He will not fail us or abandon us. An anchor secures a vessel. An anchor causes something to be fixed in place. An anchor causes something to feel attached or secure. An anchor provides support. An anchor provides stability. An anchor causes something to be immovable. Jesus Christ is our Anchor. In Him, we can remain stable. In Him, we can remain fixed and immovable. In Him, there is security. In Him, there is support. When we are anchored in Christ, it does not matter how strong the storm rages. We can hold tight to the Lord, Who will not allow us to drown. "When you pass through the waters, I *will* be with you; And through the rivers, they shall not overflow you..." (Isaiah 43:2).

The Lord is with us in every storm of life that we face. A storm can be frightening and unpredictable. A storm can be disturbing. The storms of life are inevitable. We all go through storms. We all face difficult seasons where it looks like we may drown, where it looks like we can't get through it. But with Christ as our Anchor, not only can we make it through the difficulty, but we will come out better than before because the Lord is our support. He bears the weight of our burdens. He keeps us from weakening. He keeps us from falling. He keeps us from sinking. He holds us up. It is not by might nor by power, but it is by His Spirit that we are able to make it through the storms of life. It is by His Spirit that we are not driven to despair, even in our greatest times of distress.

Without an anchor to keep us afloat and steady, storms can be overwhelmingly stressful and all-consuming. An anchor holds a vessel in place. Jesus Christ is our Anchor that keeps us fixed and in place. Jesus Christ is our Anchor when the billow of the harsh waves attempts to pull us under. Jesus Christ is our Anchor when we are tired and worn down. Jesus Christ is our Anchor when we want to let go—He holds us up so we will not sink under the pressure. Jesus Christ is a mighty help to all who seek after Him and rely on Him to be the Source of their strength.

*To God Be the Glory!*

# About the Author

Nikki St.Clair is the founder of Encouragement Through the Word of God, a Christian ministry Facebook page. Nikki's mission for the Facebook page is to encourage and uplift God's people in the truth of God's Word. Nikki discovered her love of writing at the age of seven years old. She enjoyed writing poetry and fiction stories. After Nikki gave her life to Christ, the Lord's purpose for her life was revealed, and her desire for writing became geared toward lifting up the Name of Jesus and His promises to all those who trust in Him. Nikki is the mother of two sons, and they make their home in the DMV.

Printed in the USA
CPSIA information can be obtained
at www.ICGtesting.com
CBHW071302290624
10769CB00120B/649

9 798887 385396